THE BUSINESS OF FREELANCING

How to Thrive as a Freelancer

THE BUSINESS OF FREELANCING

How to Thrive as a Freelancer

CreativesAtWork, Singapore

NEW JERSEY · LONDON · SINGAPORE · BEIJING · SHANGHAI · HONG KONG · TAIPEI · CHENNAI · TOKYO

Published by

World Scientific Publishing Co. Pte. Ltd.

5 Toh Tuck Link, Singapore 596224

USA office: 27 Warren Street, Suite 401-402, Hackensack, NJ 07601

UK office: 57 Shelton Street, Covent Garden, London WC2H 9HE

British Library Cataloguing-in-Publication Data
A catalogue record for this book is available from the British Library.

THE BUSINESS OF FREELANCING
How to Thrive as a Freelancer

ISBN 978-981-122-265-8 (hardcover)
ISBN 978-981-122-420-1 (paperback)
ISBN 978-981-122-266-5 (ebook for institutions)
ISBN 978-981-122-267-2 (ebook for individuals)

For any available supplementary material, please visit
https://www.worldscientific.com/worldscibooks/10.1142/11894#t=suppl

Desk Editor: Sandhya Venkatesh

Typeset by Stallion Press
Email: enquiries@stallionpress.com

ACKNOWLEDGEMENTS

Our sincere appreciation to:

Ryan Ong
Kristen Smith
Kevin Ou
Chan Pei Ling
Danny Lee
Teo Yi-Ling
Adrian Kwong
Amerline Lee
Tan Siew Ann
Venkat Iyer

ABOUT THE CREATIVESATWORK'S TEAM

Jayce Tham, Co-founder of CreativesAtWork (CAW)

Jayce left her corporate high-flyer job in 2012 to start CreativesAtWork. Other than handling the business development aspect of the company, she is also a host to a podcast on freelancing — The Freelance Creative Exchange — a trainer and an executive producer to several TV projects and documentaries that CAW completed. In her free time, she is a mother and a tuition teacher to her son.

Fanny Tham, Co-founder of CreativesAtWork

Fanny started her media career in 2005 when she joined an independent broadcast network. Looking for a fresh start in life, she left the company in 2012 — the same year she got married. She co-founded CreativesAtWork in 2012 after she was tired from planning her wedding. Apart from the three tiny human beings she has co-created, matching freelancers to jobs gives her the greatest joy.

Loh Yen-Lyng

Having been let go from her job suddenly in 2016, Yen-Lyng found herself at a crossroads. She gave a shot at freelancing and has never turned back on her entrepreneurial road ever since. Currently involved in building the CreativesAtWork freelancers' community, she is also an avid gardener and environmentalist.

Raven Lim

Since starting as a production assistant in the television, Raven alternated between freelancing and full-time position throughout her entire career. As audience viewing habits switched to digital, she witnessed the slow decline of the broadcast industry. So she returned to freelancing and pivoted into creating online content and project management. An avid podcaster, she is also the producer behind CreativesAtWork's Freelance Creative Exchange podcast.

Kyle Ong

A self-dubbed "Creative Swiss Army Knife", Kyle has spent the past seven years as a freelancer working on video and photo projects for brands such as Nikon, DBS, Singtel, Starhub and Sunsilk ranging from directing, production to post-production. As a creative with CreativesAtWork, Kyle is involved in many of CreativesAtWorks' initiatives.

CONTENTS

CHAPTER 1

INTRODUCTION TO FREELANCING

1.1 INTRODUCTION (WHY WE MADE THIS BOOK)

Freelancing is one of the fastest growing career paths for young people today. It is a response to what they see as the overly structured work environment of previous generations. They are bolder than previous freelancing generations, taking the reins of their careers in their hands. They are freelancing full-time, across borders, industries and occupations. With rapid changes in the economy, technology and work cultures, we see that even those who are more accustomed to a fixed office environment turn to freelancing or risk being left behind.

One of their biggest challenges is connecting with companies who need their services. Conversely, companies constantly face the challenge of finding good, proven, project-based talent for their initiatives. In 2012, CreativesAtWork was set up to be that essential link, bringing together the freelancer and the employer for media projects across Asia.

We connect talented freelancers to project owners with our matchmaking and project management services. With a strong network of media freelancers, CreativesAtWork provides a complete solution to every project owner's media needs and requirements. Since our inception, we have built a network of over 1,500 specialists in the media industry and completed more than SGD$10 million worth of projects.

The COVID-19 era shows us that the future of work is here. More projects and less budget mean that selecting the right person for the right project is imperative to success. Companies — from large Multi-National Corporations to Small Middle Enterprises — have less wiggle room than ever before. We believe creative freelancers will play a pivotal role in helping large corporations, SMEs or start-up companies to manage their internal resources and enable the use of exceptional project-based talent that would otherwise not be economically feasible to bring on board. Most importantly, during times of uncertain market conditions, they enable businesses to maximise performance across peaks and troughs in demand.

We hope through this book, it will bring about more awareness of the lesser known profession called "freelancer" and generates the next wave of "Future Leaders" with entrepreneurial and self-employed mindsets.

If you have not started your freelancing career yet, there are many things you can do to prepare yourself before you jump in. For those who have already started freelancing, we hope you find these tips useful too.

1.2 SO WHAT IS FREELANCING ALL ABOUT?

Freelancing is not always the easy, laid back lifestyle that people believe. It is challenging, many times more so than being an employee. You do not have the support of co-workers, a boss or a training team, so it is up to you to keep yourself and your business on track. Being a freelancer requires a lot of grit. But just like with everything, this mindset is something you can develop!

On the surface, a freelancer is someone who works on a contract basis. But the real differences are seen when you check under the hood — mindset, lifestyle, and skills that would differentiate the freelancer from a regular employee. As a freelancer, you will find yourself having to make many decisions that most employees take for granted such as invoicing, negotiating your pay (constantly), even where and when you work, just to name a few. All these might seem small, but they do add up the mental load that many will crumble under.

So every time we speak to a person who comes to us looking for advice on freelancing this is the first thing we tell them — you have to be mentally and emotionally prepared to take on this load. Not everything will be perfect, but you will learn to cope and improve along the way.

Luckily for you, we have compiled a ton of good tips here to help you navigate your way and skip some potholes many have stumbled over!

1.3 TYPES OF FREELANCERS

Decide what type of freelancer you want to be. Do you want to work from home, completely on your own? Or would you rather still work in an office?

If you would still like to work in an office setting, consider doing contract work. You will go into the office like any other employee, but you are only bound to the company for the length of your contract. This will play a part in how you set up your company later on.

We can divide freelancers into four general types (these may not be the categories you have heard of before!)

- Pure freelancers
- Contract workers
- Interim freelancers
- Artisans

1.3.1 *Pure Freelancers*

These freelancers often work for multiple clients at the same time. They do not have any obligation to be in an office. They adhere to deadlines, but when and how they work is entirely up to them.

These freelancers have almost total freedom. They can work from a café in Amsterdam, or in their shorts at home. But they do need to have a lot of self-discipline, as they are totally unsupervised.

1.3.2 *Contract Workers*

These freelancers turn up at the office and keep the same hours as a regular employee but they are working on a contract, just like other freelancers. Some consultants work this way, as do many specialised engineers and programmers. For these freelancers, it may not be possible to work for multiple clients at once.

1.3.3 *Interim Freelancers*

Some freelancers do not intend to stay that way. An example would be a contract worker who wants to be considered for a permanent position. Interim freelancers need to work on other areas, such as fitting in well with the corporate culture to get a permanent position.

1.3.4 *Artisans*

Artisans see their work more as a calling or art form (or craft) than a job. Financial gain is not their sole concern. Whether their medium is photography, writing, painting, etc., it is important that they derive personal satisfaction from the project. These freelancers need to pick their clients carefully; otherwise they could end up working for someone who is too controlling, or who cannot appreciate their work.

1.4 PROS & CONS OF FREELANCING

1.4.1 *Benefits of Being a Freelancer*

There are many benefits of being a freelancer. But the one that we most often hear is freedom. The freedom to be able to choose what project you want to work on, the freedom to choose how you want to work and where you want to work and the freedom to decide what you need to do when you need to do, it sounds very appealing especially to the younger generation. This is what drives most people to be a freelancer.

For some, freelancing provides an opportunity to work outside of an office. You can hang out with friends till midnight, come home, and then start work (if you are a night owl and party animal). You can work from a spa in Bali or be backpacking over the Andes during your work week.

Another advantage of freelancing is that you develop a strong network of contacts. Due to the nature of freelancing, you will inadvertently in your normal course of business get in touch with many other people whether they are your clients, your co-workers in one of the freelance projects or just random people you meet at networking events. Most freelancers will agree that they need a strong network of contacts to continue their trade.

A third advantage to freelancing is subtle, but important: freelancing does not allow you to stagnate. You have to keep finding new clients. That means developing your skills, maintaining your network, and upgrading or developing new services and products. We have often seen employees in their 40s or 50s who have a hard time when they are made redundant — many have become out of touch with what the job market demands. Freelancers are forced to keep pace and always be at the forefront of change.

A freelancer can be choosy and select desirable jobs, while avoiding the less appealing ones. This may come at a cost of lower earnings. We know several musicians who outright refuse to play certain types of music or at certain venues, even if it means earning less.

Freelancers who are less choosy often (not always) make above-average incomes. From our experience, writers who freelance instead of working for a single publication almost invariably earn more.

The final benefit we like to highlight is the easier transition from self-employed to business owner. One day, being a freelancer may no longer be sufficient. A time will come when you have more clients than you can service, and you have numerous high-level executives and directors clamouring for your time. It is an opportunity to run your own business.

This is never easy, but a freelancer will find the transition from worker to business owner easier. Freelancers already know how to deal with issues like risk and opportunity cost, how to behave like a vendor, and how to deal with fluctuating income. They have a better sense of how legal and financial paperwork is handled. Above all, they have a strong network of contacts to source clients from — in fact, many start their business with a waiting list of clients that is several months long. Hence, freelancing can also be akin to running a business. A business mindset is important in order for freelancing to be a rewarding and fulfilling journey.

1.4.2 *Challenges of Being a Freelancer*

Then we come to the difficult part of freelancing: money.

This is where it gets touchy. In our experience, freelancers can earn more than regular employees if they are not picky. This means having a craftsman mindset rather than an artist mindset.

Most likely, you'll be getting your 'salary' based on projects too. This means that many-a-time, you'll be facing unstable income. You constantly have to be on your toes, thinking about where your next paycheck is going to come from. Financial issues aside, the stress and anxiety of this turns many people away from freelancing.

Change, as much of an advantage of freelancing it is, is also a bane to some. Some people like to find a comfortable state to be in and stay there. There is no wrong in that. However, if you are a freelancer, the lifestyle of constant change that bring excitement and drive to some might also cause you stress.

With the freedom that is awarded with the lifestyle, ironically, another challenge that arises is the discipline that one must develop as a freelancer. You get to work almost any time you choose, but do you want to be working for 24 hours a day? You are unsupervised, but do you want to constantly procrastinate and deliver rushed jobs to your clients?

Being your own boss, no matter your chosen trait, you'll most likely spend a good amount of time doing business-related tasks like invoicing, pitching, canvasing, marketing, collecting payment and other administrative tasks. If you were working in a large company before, you'll most likely be used to another person or department doing these for you. However, being a one-man show, these tasks will fall on you now. These are dreaded but necessary tasks for any business.

Freelancing can also be a lonely road a lot of times. There are usually no co-workers, no water cooler chit-chat, no lunch buddies. These might seem irrelevant but many miss the social aspect and the commiserative feeling of working in a company with a team, with everyone around you moving towards a common goal. There are substitutes for this which we will touch on later. However, it is still something that does not come as naturally as when you have a team you're working together with while in the same room or building for 8-10 hours a day.

CHAPTER 2

STARTING OUT

In order to have a successful freelance business, it is important to start right. Many stumble upon it when they first start and find it difficult to continue. But if you start out right, you will have a higher chance of success. At CreativesAtWork, we seek to help new freelancers to make a smoother transition to start their freelance career.

2.1 BE YOUR OWN BOSS

Once you decide to be a freelancer, you should embrace and start taking the role seriously. As you are your own boss, you will have the responsibility to do what it takes to kickstart your freelance career.

Get your name out there: Tell people what you do, what you have done and what capability you have. With social media, you can almost start promotion of your own business at virtually no cost. When you create social content, it travels far. This is a great way to grow and expand your reach in the beginning. Write about what you know and share it across your social networks.

Leverage what is available to you: Be aware of grants that are available to you as a freelancer in your country. For example, as a freelancer in Singapore, you can apply for the SkillsFuture Programme and get up to SGD$500 for learning a skill useful to you. You can also leverage on various digital grants to get access to business tools such as accounting to keep your business in check.

Start even before you start: If you are still in school, take on freelance jobs. These real-world projects can help prepare you for your career and help you make the connections you will rely on later on. If you are still at your full-time job, consider taking on some freelancing projects to supplement your work if you have time. Start making those connections and gaining experience before you plunge into it full-time.

As a freelancer, you have direct control over your career. How much effort you put in will directly affect how successful you are. Yet, without management from above, it can be easy to slip into passiveness. Being proactive in your career, your business and your life will serve you well as an entrepreneur and business owner.

You can consider some of the following ways to guide you towards a more productive freelance journey.

Set goals: Consistently set appropriate goals for your freelance career to propel yourself forward. When you achieve goals, take the time to congratulate yourself. Once in a while, look back to see all of the goals you have set and achieved over the years.

Manage industry shifts: As the market changes, keep yourself proactive and change with the times. This is even more important for freelancers. Do not resist change in your industry, because it will always hold you back. Be willing to transform and stay alert so that you are always ahead of the curve rather than behind it.

Get out of ruts: If you are stuck in a situation or a position in your career you do not like, try to change something! As a freelancer, you are not tied to particular jobs, so make the effort to find something you really enjoy doing.

Upgrade skills: One of the best ways to stay relevant and working is to constantly upgrade your skills. If you can show potential clients or companies that you have taken the initiative to upskill and sharpen your knowledge of the industry on your own; it will reflect well on your capabilities.

Beat nerves: Act, despite fear! There will always be things that make you nervous. Learn to work through your fear and go after what you want.

Try new things: Have the guts to challenge the status quos and do not let negative stories dictate your trajectory! Get creative about your problems and forge new paths.

Ask outrageously: Let your creative mind be free to come up with crazy, innovative ideas and do not be afraid to propose them to clients. Think outrageously and ask outrageously. If you never ask, you will never know. If the answer is no, then you have not lost anything. If you ask and the answer is yes, then you just jumped up a level.

2.2 FINDING YOUR NICHE

Finding a niche can help you become an expert in a single industry and help you grow a sustainable business. Although it may limit your scope of clients, you may find you get paid more, get more referrals, and become more well known in your industry.

If you are in a niche that you love, you will be passionate about it and have lots of energy for the work you are doing. You will continue to get more effective and efficient at the work that you do, and you will find that you are able to be more profitable. Just make sure you devote yourself to a niche that you enjoy!

Task: Find your niche.
Start a success journal.
Take some time to evaluate patterns in your business.

- What are some jobs you have enjoyed most?
- What has been the easiest for you to do?
- What jobs have you been the proudest of?
- What has been the most lucrative?
- What brings value to your clients?
- What can you specialise in that can get you quite well known?

Write the answers down in your success journal. Keep this journal handy as we will add more into the journal.

Do you see any patterns? Are there one or two jobs that came up a lot? These may be where your greatest opportunities lie.

If you see yourself developing your skills to take on these types of jobs as your niche specialty, how can you make that happen? Where are some places you can find clients that need work like this done? Can you ask for referrals from some of your previous clients?

At the beginning of your career, you may not have much chance. However, if you know that you have a goal of entering a niche market, you can keep an eye out for these types of jobs and work in the direction of that niche while you develop your business.

2.3 GET IN THE FRAME OF MIND

As a freelancer, you are your own boss. This means you have to have self-responsibility in every sense. Everything from meeting deadlines to cleaning up messes, filing taxes, and getting hired falls on you. It is a myth that as a creative freelancer, you will be being creative all the time. You will spend at least 70 percent of your time on the administrative side of your company. Marketing, invoicing, money management, legal contracts, insurance, all take time too!

Getting into the right frame of mind is important as you are no longer a salaried employee but rather your own boss.

Gain experience: Having experience in your sector in the corporate world can be really beneficial in your freelancing career. If you are just starting out, consider taking an internship or a job for a short-term, spend an amount of time in a corporate setting. Connecting and understanding corporate structure will help you to manage your relationship with your future clients better.

Learn what you need: In the beginning, you may have to put your dreams aside for a bit to learn the skills required to get you to the top of your industry. Every professional needs to go through a learning period. This is all just part of the process. Be open-minded and prepare to learn from others.

Get involved before: If there is a particular industry or sector you want to work in, start looking for opportunities where you can meet people who are already involved. Leverage things like Facebook groups, meetup.com, LinkedIn for more opportunities.

Network, make and keep connections: Having friends in the corporate world can help you make your career sustainable because you will have connections for jobs. Even if you step out of the corporate world, keep your connections.

Join a community: As a freelancer, you will not have the guidance of a boss or co-workers. Consider joining a community of freelancers or look for a mentor to give you advice as you enter into your new career.

Task: Find a mentor.

Brainstorm some ideas about who you could ask to be your mentor. This person does not have to be exactly in your industry — it could be someone who is an entrepreneur or a freelancer in another industry. If they have developed skills that you want, they can teach you something.

Make it a goal to contact one of these people within the next week to ask if they would be willing to mentor you.

If you do not know any other freelancers or business-owners that could help you, look online. There are many social media interest groups and websites that publish blog posts daily about freelancing, creative work, and entrepreneurship. If you find a site that really connects with you, you can sign up for their newsletter and make it a habit to always read their content. In this way, you will have virtual mentorship.

2.4 DEALING WITH SETBACKS

As a creative, it can be easy to fall into the trap of complacency and lacklustre work. At times in your freelance career, you might need an extra push to stay on your creative edge. What can you do to always stay on top of your game? It could be an intensive sport, or a pep talk with your close friends or even a retreat for yourself. No matter what it is, it is good to give yourself some personal space from time to time in order to move on a longer-term journey.

2.4.1 *Cultivate Creativity*

Here are some strategies to keep your creativity up.

Be fearless with your work and your creativity. Do not be afraid to look silly, it is all about learning and gaining experience — not perfection.

If you are focused so much on the feedback and shares you get from your freelance work, take a step back and remember why you do and what you do in the first place. Do not think in terms of numbers, use your spirit to drive your work.

2.4.2 *Be a Flexible Problem Solver*

No matter how much you prepare, there will be unexpected things that come up during a project. How you deal with the fallout and maintain your timeline is what counts when these things happen.

Flexibility should be part of your mindset, as well as your engagement agreements. Learn to be agile with yourself and with your clients. When problems arise, be creative, not reactive. Take control of the situation and plan a response, rather than quickly reacting to something.

Freelancers who know how to solve problems are extremely valuable to their clients. They become almost invaluable because, without them, the client's problems are not going to get solved. If a client asks you to do something you know cannot be done, for whatever reasons, offer solutions. If you can show that you offer more than just execution, but consultation, your value goes up.

2.5 BUILD YOUR COMMUNITY

As a freelancer, you do not have the support and community of co-workers around you. You may feel that as an individual you are competing against an entire sea of other freelancers. However, by switching your perspective to see other freelancers as your community, you increase your own value by now becoming a team player that can collaborate to achieve more. You can find and build your community through networking events, meetup.com groups or online, such as on Facebook groups.

2.5.1 *How Being Part of a Community Benefits You*

Building a culture of care with your community will help you work in a harmonious industry. Share your knowledge freely about the industry, clients, and projects (within your bounds, of course) with your community. Helping others achieve greatness will help you achieve great results in the end and will form bonds that can help you in the future. When people feel that you are going out of your way to help them, they will do the same for you.

Being less competitive and more collaborative may get you more work in the end. When you can leverage your community's talents and skills, you increase your own value, as well as everyone else's. They will do the same for you!

You can also learn from your "competitor." All the best companies learn from their competitors, and you are under an obligation as a professional to stay at the cutting edge of your industry.

Remember, it is okay to ask for help! As a freelancer, you do not have the usual inter-office relationships that most workers get to enjoy. Having a community of other freelancers to turn to for advice can help elevate your level of work and take the pressure off you to work on your own.

2.6 KEEPING YOUR FINANCIAL STATS STABLE

As a creative, you may not have the strongest sense of how to handle finances. However, it is crucially important in running your business and will determine the height of your success. Before you even start your freelancing career, you should have at least six months of savings to get you through any unforeseen circumstances, like sickness, late payments, or project delays. The only constant thing for freelancing is change. Always be prepared and expect the unexpected. The current COVID-19 pandemic is a particularly good example and lesson.

There are five important guidelines to managing your finances as a freelancer.

- Windfalls offset downfalls
- What gets measured gets managed
- Build the emergency fund first
- Free work should not be free
- Know your grants

2.6.1 *Windfalls Offset Downfalls*

Say you made SGD$9,000 this month, whereas you usually make SGD$5,000 a month. The extra SGD$4,000 should not be blown as a bonus.

Instead, keep it. If the next two months are bad, the excess SGD$4,000 can be used to prop up your income. For example:

Say you make only SGD$3,000 a month for the next two months, because it is a dry spell. Your savings of SGD$4,000 can be divided between these two months, to raise your income to the norm of SGD$5,000 even when the market is bad.

Making your income consistent helps with financial planning.

2.6.2 *What Gets Measured Gets Managed*

You need a proper system of invoices and receipts. And even if you do not want to use Excel, you *must* record the transactions somewhere. There are also many free online accounting tools out there that can help you with invoicing and tracking of payments.

Legal reasons aside, you could miss payments or overspend if you do not keep records. You would also need to have proper documentation or records for tax filing purposes.

Once you have multiple clients, all of whom pay on different dates, you are liable to get confused. It is time consuming — and a little embarrassing — to call up your entire client list and tell them you do not know if they have paid you.

It is also easier to overspend if you are not clear on your cashflow.

2.6.3 *Build the Emergency Fund First*

Your first goal is to build up an emergency fund. If you do not already have six months' worth of income as your savings, then you should build up the fund. Set aside at least 20 percent of your monthly income to go into this fund, until it reaches the adequate amount. This removes the need for expensive loans and helps you to deal with any unforeseen circumstances.

2.6.4 *Free Work Should not be Free*

If work does not have a monetary benefit, it should pay you in some other way. Will doing the work introduce you to other important clients? Will it get you media attention? Is there equity involved if you are giving a lot of time to a start-up?

Do not do free work if there is little or no benefit (with the exception of charity).

Work out how much you make an hour and use it to determine if free work has a commensurate benefit. For example:

Say you get paid around SGD$200 an hour for most projects. You are asked to do something for free, which will get you mentioned on the radio. It will take you five hours.

You will then have to decide if being mentioned on air is worth (5 hours x SGD$200) SGD$1,000 to you.

2.6.5 *Know Your Grants*

Be on the lookout for government or corporate grants that could help you. In Singapore, the SkillsFuture Agency is established to help Singaporeans to upskill and upgrade themselves. The Singapore Government provides SkillsFuture Credit for all Singaporeans to use to offset against programmes under SkillsFuture. So, you can use the SGD$500 SkillsFuture Credit to learn the accounting skills you may need.

2.6.5.1 *Financial tracking*

Keeping your business finance accounts in order is an important part of running your business and for:

- sustainability and longevity of the business
- tax and account records
- tracking business trends
- ensuring collectibles and payables are properly accounted for

Without proper financial tracking, you will have little idea of how your business is actually doing. If you want your business to succeed in the long run, set yourself up for success by being as professional as possible with your finances from the beginning.

When tax season comes, especially if you have a company, your accounts must be in order. Even if you are filing personally, it will be a massive help to already have your income, business expenses and write-offs accounted for.

Each month keep track of your expenses and income. If you keep track of it over the whole year, you can see trends in your business and your expenses. This can help you with financial planning for the next year.

As a freelancer, it is important to track your invoices, payments, and money out. Make sure to retain invoices, receipts, and other documents throughout the year to support your business records and accounts (profits and losses). As a general rule, save your records and supporting documents for five years before disposing of them. This might vary slightly by country.

Manual bookkeeping, Excel spreadsheets, software like Mind Your Own Business (MYOB), online tools like QuickBooks Online, and applications like ZOHO Books or Wave Invoice are all ways you can track your business finances. Some of them have extra perks, like sending out automatic invoices.

Because you are your own business, you can decide when your 12-month accounting period ends. You can pick any date that serves you, but most people choose to end their fiscal year on 31 December. This may vary, depending on when your country's tax season starts. At the end of your accounting period, you should prepare a statement of accounts that includes a profit and loss statement and a balance sheet.

The most important thing in business finance is to ensure that your cashflow is higher than your expenses. If it is not, first, try to increase your income. If you cannot increase your income, think about ways you can lower your expenses.

2.6.5.2 *Taxes*

As you are your own employer, you are responsible for submitting your taxes. No-one will be deducting taxes from your paycheck as you go. As each country's tax laws are different, it is best to do some research of your own to find out how to best handle paying taxes as a freelancer, self-employed person, or independent contractor in your country.

However, there are some general rules of thumb any freelancer can apply.

(a) Learn about your country's tax laws concerning freelancers. A Google search or a visit to your country's .gov page should help get you started. If you feel you need more help, reach out to a tax advisor or someone who has already been in the freelancing industry for a while in your country.

Note: Hiring a tax accountant is very advisable. Although they can be expensive, they can often save you money by informing you of possible deductions. Tax laws are complicated, and now that you are your own employer, it is essential you have someone on your side who can explain it to you. If you have a tax accountant, they will advise you on what to set aside.

(b) **Decide whether you want to charge taxes on top of your services or have it included in your price.** This will make a difference on how you price yourself to begin with. The amount of taxes you charge or consider as part of your fee will depend on which country you live in. For the United States, experts recommend setting aside 30–40 percent for taxes. For Singapore, this will most likely be much lower, around 10 percent or 17 percent if you set up a corporate entity.

(c) **Keep track of all your income and expenses.** Keeping track of your receipts is especially important for tax season. As a freelancer or contractor, your expenses will be tax-deductible for your business. Whether you buy a new computer for writing, rent out a co-working space, or take a taxi to see a client, any expense legitimately connected to your business is tax-deductible in most countries.

(d) **Save or pay-as-you-go.** You definitely want to avoid a big bill at the end of tax season that you are not prepared for. Every time you are paid, take money out and put it into a tax account. In some countries, you can pay tax estimates quarterly, so tax season is not such a huge burden.

Note: For most countries, there is a threshold you must cross before paying any taxes if necessary. For example, in Singapore, you can make up to SGD$20,000 a year before needing to pay taxes.

The main thing to remember is that you are solely responsible for paying your taxes, with no reminders. Make sure you are setting yourself up for success by being aware of all the requirements and recommendations from your particular country.

2.6.5.3 *Other considerations*

While it is important to always have a financial contingency plan, try not to fall into the habit of cutting costs in order to sustain your business. Be creative rather than reactive and look for other avenues to make income instead, such as passive income.

Depending on the country you live in, it may be good to join an interest group or a union. Interest groups will provide you with emotional support and can be a good avenue for job referrals. Unions will look out for your interests, keep you protected, and provide support.

Tracking your finances will take your freelancing business to another level and help ensure you succeed. If you truly feel you cannot handle your financial tracking and planning, it is a good idea to hire someone to do it for you.

2.7 TIME MANAGEMENT

As a freelancer, it is up to you to balance your working time and personal time. This is one of the biggest perks of being a freelancer: managing your own schedule. Your working hours are completely up to you, but it may not be as easy as you think to handle your own time, especially as you build your business. Sacrifices will be necessary, but keep in mind the true costs.

Time is the one thing we can never earn back! And thus, it is of essence to a freelancer.

Here are a few things you need to work out at the start of your journey.

- **Establish your work hours.** If you only want to work a 40-hour week, then list all your projects and see that they fit into that time frame. If they fall under, you can take more jobs; if they exceed it, you run the risk of missing deadlines.
- **If one goes on, one goes off.** A simple, but effective method, is to just list your daily responsibilities. Whenever you take on a new job, a previous one must be removed or resolved.
- **Pick effective hours.** Part of the joy of freelancing is that you work on your own schedule. If you are super effective after 7 pm, but a complete zombie at 7 am, then go ahead and work nights. Work when you are at your mental peak.
- **Use group project software.** If your client uses a system like Asana, Slack, or Trello, request to be a part of it. You are not in the office and they cannot see what you are doing — these systems ensure you coordinate better with the client's employees and face fewer lapsed deadlines.
- **Get in the habit of using Video Conferencing tools.** Systems like Zoom, Google Meet, Skype or Facetime are invaluable to freelancers. Before scheduling a face-to-face meet, ask yourself if it is absolutely necessary. If not, save yourself the travel time, and request a conference call.
- **Track how long it takes you to do a project.** This will help you with your billing if you charge by the hour and when you move into charging per project. It will help you figure out how much time you need per client and project and help inform how many clients you can take on at once.

As you track your time, look at the things that take the longest or stop your workflow. How can you reduce the amount of time these things take?

- **Track how long you can stay focused:** If you can only look at your design screen for two hours at a time before you stop being effective, break up your work hours. Make sure that you honour your time and do not push yourself beyond your limits.
- **Spend time doing other creative things:** Having a creative outlet that is completely unrelated to your industry can be helpful in releasing stress and keeping creative energy flowing. Since it is not related to what you do to pay the bills, there should be no pressure on the end result.

2.7.1 *Schedule Balancing Hacks*

Here are some hacks you can consider:

(a) **Create to-do lists properly:** Have a task list for each day that fills up your day realistically, not with way too many things to complete. Know that if you need to add something to this list, then something needs to come off the list also. This will keep your working hours consistent.

(b) **Give yourself time for self-care:** Well-being is important to freelancers. If you do not feel well, you do not perform as well and this directly impacts your livelihood. Sick days are not paid when you are freelancing — your mental and physical health should be a top priority. Remember to give yourself time to rest and relax. Mark these times off as specific non-working hours — do not answer emails or phone calls about work.

(c) **Work when you are most effective:** Since you can pick your own hours, choose to work the hours where you are most effective. If you work well after 7 pm but are a zombie before 7 am, work nights and enjoy your lazy mornings!

(d) **Outsource small jobs:** Do not be afraid to outsource small jobs that take up a lot of time. Let us say you need to deliver prints to your client's office. Instead of taking an hour to make the trip (worth whatever your hourly rate is), hire someone to do it for you. There are many apps and sites where you can hire people for menial tasks.

(e) Learn to say no: Saying no will be one of the most powerful things you will learn as a freelancer. You might need to take every job you can in the beginning, but as you grow your business, you will need to discern what is good for you, your time, and your brand.

(f) Have designated email hours. Give yourself select hours (no more than two a day) which are dedicated entirely to sending and answering emails. If you do not, you will waste precious time by forgetting to send or reply to emails. You will also interrupt your workflow by constantly stopping to check your mail. A good approach is to have an email hour at the start and end of the workday.

(g) Outsource the small jobs. Some jobs are simple but time consuming, such as tying ribbons on the custom wedding invites you have made or delivering a thumb drive to the client's office. Outsource these small jobs if it frees up time for bigger ones. There are sites like TaskAmigo, where you can find temporary helpers.

All of these things will help you balance your schedule, but the thing that will help you the most is understanding why you work, when you work and why you do not when you do not. Building your business must be a priority, but you must know what else is important to your happiness.

Task: What are your time non-negotiables?

In your success journal, write down things that you cannot afford to miss in your life. It could be things like eating dinner with your family every night or making it to your favourite sports game on the weekends.

Remember these things as you balance your schedule — as non-negotiables, they should never be infringed upon! If they are, it is time to have a look at redoing your schedule.

2.7.2 *Planning Time Effectively*

Freelance is 70 percent business, 30 percent creativity. Behind every successful freelancer are countless hours of marketing and managing their business. However, you most likely will not be getting paid unless you are working on a project for a client. This means how you spend your time is crucially important.

When planning your weeks and days, consider how much time you have to work, and then consider that many of those hours will not actually be spent working on projects for clients. Here are some steps to take to ensure good time management.

(a) **Split your time** between acquiring clients, filing your accounts, upgrading your skills, etc., depending on what is most important to your business goals. Observe what in your business needs the most time at the moment and be agile, willing to prioritise different things, week to week.

  Learning to juggle your clients, your marketing, and upgrading your skills will take some time. In the beginning, you may have to work long hours, doing all three at once!

(b) **Create a realistic to-do list each day.** Give yourself a mental pat on the back each time you complete something — you do not have a boss or co-workers to motivate you, so you have to be your own encouragement!

(c) **Make working hours for yourself and stick to them.** Just because you are a freelancer, does not mean you need to be free all the time. If you have a set schedule, then you can refer to that when people ask you to make dates and you do not have time. You are allowed to be fluid, but realistic and honest when you review how your time management has been. What works for you?

(d) **Treat it like a real workday.** Even though you may be able to work from home in your pyjamas, this might not be the best for your business schedule. As this is your business, approach your workdays like real workdays — get dressed, have a working hour and break schedule, and have a set stopping time.

(e) **Work when you work best.** Having set work hours is a good strategy for managing your time, but this does not mean you have to follow regular office hours. If you work best after dinner, work nights. If you get scatter-brained after lunch and then have to pick your kids up at 2 pm, work in the mornings. Leverage your schedule to work for you.

(f) **Have email hours.** Schedule two hours or less for emails in your day. You do not want to lose time or money forgetting to write people back or interrupt your workflow to check your email. A good best practice is to spend one hour before work and one hour after work to check emails.

(g) **Use a project management tool** like Asana or basecamp to help you manage your business, your projects and your communications with your clients. This can help you keep track of your schedule and your projects. In some apps, you can synchronise communication with clients, eliminating the need to email back and forth.

(h) **Create processes with steps.** After you do business for a while or complete a particular type of project many times, you will start to see where you repeat steps on a daily or per project basis. Things like having your client sign a contract and then sending it back to them will always be part of your operations. You can "project process" templates on apps such as Asana that you can copy and paste for each new project that outlines each step you need to take. This way, you will not waste time thinking about what you need to do next.

(i) **Create time-saving collateral.** This could be things like screen grabs, standard videos and email templates explaining the workflow and next steps for new clients, surveys about clients' needs, or e-brochures about your capabilities and offerings. Anything that you do often that can be put in a template will save you time!

(j) **Cut out time–wasting.** Your time is valuable, and as a freelancer, you are often not getting paid unless you are producing something. So, make sure to keep meetings with clients, short and concise. See that the direction of the meeting is fruitful, otherwise, cut it short.

(k) **Do not double-book yourself.** As a freelancer, you are responsible for planning your own schedule. Be careful not to double-book yourself. You may not have the bandwidth to complete projects and complete them well.

(l) Plan ahead. As a freelancer, you always have to think ahead to avoid lag time between jobs. You may be knee-deep in a project now, but where will you be when the project ends in two weeks? Take time to network and schedule jobs *ahead of time* so you do not end up without work.

(m) Use any lag-time wisely. When work is slow and you do not have many gigs, use your time to do something else productive for your business, like updating your website, upgrading your skills, or looking at your budget.

In the beginning, everything — from negotiating to finishing projects to invoicing — will take longer. As your business develops, you will learn how to streamline.

2.8 WORKSHEET

Let try out some activities now.

<u>Introduction Task #1</u>

Keep updating your "success journal". By doing this exercise and keeping all your important knowledge here, you're telling yourself that success is inevitable.

Continue updating the journal as you progress reading the book.

<u>Introduction Task #2</u>

Define what success is to you in your journal. Here are some prompt questions to help you get started.

What does a successful life look like to you?

Do you want to have a lot of money, or is having a lot of free time more important to you?

What does your ideal workday look like?

Do you want to be famous/well-known?

What are the goals of your business and your work?

Do you eventually want to scale or sell your business?

When do you want to retire?

The last question is especially important when writing your business plan. To figure out how to get "there" (your goal) you need to know where you are going.

In addition to figure out your business goal, you should also figure out why your goal is what it is! Understanding your motivations will help you make decisions in your career journey.

CHAPTER 3

MARKETING YOURSELF AND GETTING CLIENTS

3.1 HOW TO MARKET YOURSELF

As a small business owner, marketing is important — if you are the best at what you do but no one knows about you, then how can you do your job? There are many parts to marketing and branding yourself well, but the first step is to think about *how* and *why* you want to position yourself.

As you are the face of your company, your branding should match who you are as a person. A brand is a promise to your audience — it tells them what to expect when they are working with you. All of your online content — your Facebook, your Instagram, your LinkedIn, and your website, should reflect your personality, your style, and your values.

The other side of this is that the way you brand yourself will affect who wants to do business with you. One of the best things about being a freelancer is deciding who you want to work with and do business with. If you know what is important to you, you can attract people that value those same things, and your life will become easier. Working with people who have the same values as you will result in longer term relationships and needless to say, more fruitful ones as well.

Getting to the core of your values will help you figure out how you run your business, market yourself, and produce your deliverables. The most common and cheaper way to start is to build up your online presence.

3.1.1 *Positioning Yourself*

Before you get into how you will market your services, think about how you want to position yourself, using your values, personal attributes, and experience. This will determine how you tell your story.

What is your unique value proposition? What can you do that no one else can do? Are you more playful with your writing than your competitors? Can you turn around projects fast? Do you have mass amounts of time to work on projects right now?

The clearer you are about who you are and what you do, the easier it will be for clients to see your value to their project.

When thinking of value, you can either offer exclusivity, relationship and customisation, efficiency, or novelty and innovation. However, it is only possible to really use two of these at any given time and they must stay consistent with clients.

Being **exclusive** means that you charge higher than the market price and you pick which clients you want to work for. This will probably only come when you have more experience in your niche.

Having a **relationship** with your clients means that you understand them and their needs and that you can customise the product you sell to them to fit those needs. It also means that you have *time* to really get to know them.

Efficiency means you can get the job done faster than the next guy, and for less money. If you have a way to truly be efficient — then you can market yourself this way. If you are sacrificing your rate of pay to be more efficient, then you should not play this game. Getting paid enough to live will just get harder and harder.

Position yourself in a way that you can continue to be successful, even in the era of freelancing marketplaces like Fiverr and Upwork. These marketplaces are platforms where freelancers from overseas can provide good quality work for as little as USD$5 or USD$10. Instead of being discouraged by these trends, think creatively about how and where you can position yourself to still make a living. Remember, if your unique value proposition is strong, you will not have a problem earning what you are worth.

Task: In your success journal, write down your unique value proposition. It may be something like: I use my experience in gardening to create beautiful digital art using floral colours and a blend of natural and imagined shapes. This provides clients looking for innovative artwork with pieces that are unique, yet somehow familiar.

3.1.2 *Branding and Storytelling*

Everyone has a personal brand, whether we like it or not. What people say about you when you are not around, what you tell people about yourself, and what comes up when you google yourself are all part of your personal brand. Good examples of individuals with strong personal branding are Gary Vaynerchuk (also known as Gary Vee) who is now one of the most successful marketers in the world and has attracted a huge loyal fan base. And Oprah Winfrey, her personal brand is worth an estimated $2.5 billion according to Forbes.

Branding is telling your story and attracting the right people to you. Branding is about how people remember you after you leave a networking event. Branding is *not* about creating a fake image and selling it.

Having a clear and compelling story is important so you can (1) differentiate yourself from the hoard of other freelancers, (2) build relationships with clients and potential clients, and (3) increase your searchability for the services you offer.

If you look at any wildly successful brand, it is not about what they sell, it is about what they believe and the ideas they sell. People do not buy what you do, but "why" you do it. Knowing what you stand for is the most important thing in developing your brand and your business and this should show in your brand story.

Building your brand is easy when you know what steps to take. What is difficult is deciding what you want to be known for. What messages you put out will determine what types of people are attracted to you and what types of people you will work with.

Task: Ask yourself: What can you do for the world? What do you want to be known for? Who do you really want to work with? Write your answers down in your success journal.

3.1.3 *Your Brand Story*

Now that you have an idea of where you want to position yourself, what your unique value propositions are, and who you want to work with, it is time to formulate your brand story. Your personal story and the message behind your business.

A brand story can be your strategy for everything. It is all the stories of your company — the underlying narrative — why your company came about, who you serve, your values, how you communicate with your customers and partners, etc. It is the map for all the communications you put out and how you craft your presence. Remember that everything you do will adds to your brand story — so keep to your original values and purpose to make your story stronger.

Your brand story can be written on your social media and/or website or just something you use behind the scenes for all your branding and marketing efforts. Your website should reflect who you are as a person, through your brand story. People hire those who they know, like and trust. If you can connect with people through your brand, you will find people love to work with you.

Use your storytelling to convert people into customers — create awareness with a story or blog, get readers onto your website and use your website story to show you are an expert. Then, convert them with a service that connects with them.

Hint: Your "About page" is the second most visited page on your website, and it will convert if your branding is strong.

Task: Write your brand story in your success journal or on your computer. Your story should introduce you, show how it is relevant to your customers, and then invite them to be a part of your story.

When writing, think about what makes you a bit different or what you know that most people do not know in your industry. What do you love about your industry? What makes you frustrated? What do you see that is outdated? What drives you, what makes you more qualified than others?

One way to structure your origin story is to explain what your problem or your industry's problem was and explain how what you do is solving it.

Another way to write it is to tell the big "Aha!" moment that led you to where you are now. For example, you might write about how you knew you wanted to go into web design after learning some HTML to edit your MySpace when you were younger.

Here are some tips for writing a strong brand story.

1. **Write from the heart** and do not make it overly intellectual. Use emotion when writing and connect it to where you are now. Use your story to show your passion for your work.

2. **Show your values** — people with values similar to yours will be attracted to you through your story. This also allows your clients to decide if you are a good fit for them.

3. **Be specific!** This will add texture to your story and attract people with similar interests to you.

4. **Zoom in on moments.** When you zoom in on moments and use details, make sure that you tell your reader or listener why this is important and link it to your values.

5. **Be persuasive and believable.** Your brand story should be true, and it should excite you. If you are passionate about what you do, then this should be really easy.

6. **Know who you want to work with.** Who are they? What do they enjoy doing? What sort of language would they identify

with? Create content that will enable them to identify with you. For example, if you are a music producer, including what your muses are may strike a chord with those who like similar sounds.

Tip: If you are just starting out and do not feel very comfortable yet, use this to your advantage in your story. Be humble with your journey and share your story as you go along. In this way, people can buy into your story by seeing how much you have improved over the years.

3.2 BUILDING ONLINE REPUTATION

Being a freelancer means marketing your own services. There is no sales team, PR team, and marketing team to sell your service for you. You will have to do it yourself. Now that you have your brand story. What should you do next?

These are some options you can consider to build your online presence.

- **Social Media Channels** — Create your company's social media channels. You can use your company name or your personal name. Social media platforms like Facebook, LinkedIn, Instagram are easier to set up and are useful to profile your business.
- **Website or Blogging** — Start a blog to talk about your service or product. Post your articles on Facebook, Twitter, or even see if other bloggers will syndicate your work. This is a good way to get the message out about yourself.
- **Offer deals to entire associations** — Find an organisation closely related to your work and give them a bulk promotion. For example, you could offer to create websites at a special price for everyone in a particular insurance organisation, or an art movement. This is faster than approaching people one at a time.

- **Comment on relevant issues** — Visit forums, or write in to newspapers and magazines, to comment on areas relevant to your work. If you are a musician, for example, weigh in (politely) on issues of the local music scene. Be vocal and known.
- **Demonstrate your expertise** — If you are a tax agent, for example, you could get some interest by making a YouTube video about how to lower business taxes. This also positions you as an expert.
- **Get someone to do it for you** — This is not recommended for new freelancers, as it is expensive and deprives you of learning how to market yourself. But you can engage Marketing or Public Relations firms (costs may range from USD 2000 a month to well over USD 7000) to raise your profile.

To create your online presence is only the first step. On an ongoing basis, you need to build up your online reputation so that potential clients will be attracted to do business with you. Here are three aspects to building a solid online reputation:

- Congruence
- Characterising element
- Association

Congruence means your online persona — on Facebook, Instagram, Twitter, etc. — must not run contrary to what you claim to do. If you are a freelance writer, for example, your Facebook post should not read *"Lol, you're seeing mi new post."* Nor should you be a fitness coach with a dozen Instagram pictures of you smoking.

A **characterising element** is something you want clients to associate with you. Bloggers like Dawn Yang and Xiaxue promote many things besides fashion, but fashion is still their primary draw. Your online persona should not be scattered — people should associate it with your line of work (e.g. finance, illustration, photography).

Association is visible in the online world. This refers to whose articles you share, who often appears on your Facebook wall, and who you may have got into an online spat with. You will be associated with the three or four online personas you interact with most, so pick them carefully.

Task: You want your branding to reflect your values so you can attract those who have the same values as you. Likewise, your online personality should match your real personality. Your clients should have a seamless experience between who you really are and what you market yourself as.

In your success journal, write down three to six of your core values — things like integrity, passion, empathy.

Then, write down three words that can describe you — things like bubbly or self-motivated. Brainstorm some ways you can display these things across all platforms you utilise to market your business. If you cannot think of any, that is okay, we will come back to this later.

Next, write down the types of people you would like to work with and the types of jobs you would like to do. Maybe you are really passionate about writing investigative journalism. Who are the publishers that are already producing this type of work? If you do not have any solid ideas yet, you can write down more general qualities, like open–minded or top tier. Keep this somewhere and whenever you are putting out content on your own channels be sure to take it out and see if it is still relevant.

3.2.1 *Social Media*

Social media is an important avenue for any marketing effort, including marketing your freelancing services. For certain industries, your social media will be bigger than your business card or your portfolio. You should use your social media to tell your story and expand your reach and awareness. However, you do not have to use all social media channels to do this.

Here are some tips for growing a strong social media presence for *your* business.

(a) **See that your online presence has congruence**, even on your personal pages. If you are a health coach, do not post 10 photos of you smoking on your Facebook. If you are a writer, see that even your personal posts do not have silly mistakes or bad wording.

(b) **Always have the story and the tone first** when storytelling, no matter what the platform. Let your content speak, rather than changing yourself for the platform. Your brand voice should not change from stream to stream.

(c) **Be professional.** Take yourself seriously and others will too. After all, you are a business professional.

(d) **Plan your posts.** Think about your target audience and how you will get your content to them, rather than posting random content with no direction.

(e) **Use the correct social media platform for your business.** If you are a photographer, use Instagram. If you are a writer, use LinkedIn to showcase your articles.

(f) **Focus on engagement.** When it comes to social media marketing, having likes is not the real measure of engagement. Make sure that you are posting content that people are interacting with either by commenting on it or sharing it.

(g) Be responsive. When someone reaches out to you on social media or another platform about a potential job, respond right away. Be engaging and avoid missing out on any potential gigs!

(h) Stay consistent. Think about who your audience is and create for them consistently. Eventually, you will get noticed.

(i) Do not worry about critiques through comments. Be confident in what you are creating. Not everyone is going to love your work because we all have different tastes. But if you like it, be confident and proud of your work, even if it is not perfect.

(j) Find potential clients by searching the platform for who might need your services and reaching out to them. However, make sure your social media looks professional and helpful before you start using a platform to find clients.

If you are using social media platforms as your primary source of finding clients, then you will need to build up a solid brand and expand your following first. This can be a daunting task, but if you follow the steps we learned, you can build a strong reputation and following online.

3.2.2 Portfolio

A portfolio is a collection of your works that can help you to attract new clients or score your dream job. Publishing your most compelling work samples creates a valuable promotional tool that will expand your professional opportunities. When it comes to proving yourself professionally, it is important to show *and* tell. This is also the first level of assessment that we, at CreativesAtWork, used to qualify our freelancers.

3.2.2.1 *Building a strong portfolio*

Your portfolio is a project in itself — as a creative, use this space to show off what you can do. If you are a writer, include powerful titles and captions. If you are a graphic designer, the portfolio itself should show off your talent.

Your brand story should stay visible throughout your portfolio as well. Remember your values, unique proposition, and desired client base. Your tone, design, and projects in your portfolio should reflect all of these things. If you have a skill that not many people have, make sure you highlight that. If you market yourself as efficient, include timelines to show off how quickly you can get things done.

This is not the space just to show *what* you can do, but also *how* you do it. Create space or time in your portfolio to explain how you approached projects, what your challenges were, and how you solved problems. You can also speak about how you worked with a team to complete a project. This gives potential clients a look into what they can expect when working with you and shows off your problem–solving skills.

Ensure your portfolio has a clear focus and niche. Although you may be able to do many different types of work, showcasing your specialty will be the most effective in gaining new clients. You may want to even create multiple portfolios with different focuses if you want to go after different types of jobs.

Make sure your portfolio is impeccable before posting it online or sending it out. Any small mistake could cost you a potential client's trust. You can reach out to your peers or your community of free-lancers or a mentor to help you check through your portfolio and suggest improvements or even edits.

At the beginning of your career, you might not have enough work done to build a good portfolio. It is okay to mock-up for imaginary clients to showcase what your capabilities are. Likewise, if you want to get a particular type of job that you do not have any experience in, you can create a mock-up or a prototype.

It is possible that you may need to work for free to build your port-folio in the beginning, but this is not something you should do often. If you decide to do it for free, make sure the trade-offs are beneficial to you. Make sure that you are part of the creation and design process. You want to show that you can produce quality work with your vision.

If you do something for free, see it as a marketing cost and keep it to a bare minimum. Let the client know what the scope of the pro-ject is that you will be doing for free and do not go over that. When you have completed the part you agreed to do for free, you can offer to do more for a price. Do not get into the habit of doing work free of charge — your time is valuable.

The goal of the portfolio is to show your potential client who you are and your values, it is also to get the potential assignment that you are always looking for to level up your skills. Hence, it is not just a one-off exercise, it is an ongoing process of tweaking, refin-ing and enhancing your portfolio, putting in relevant works, tak-ing out non-relevant works etc. Sending potential clients to a place online where they can interact with your previous work and peak inside how you work is a powerful tool in gaining a client's interest and trust.

3.3 NETWORKING

Your network is one of the most important parts of your freelancing business. Through your network, you will get jobs, grow your knowledge, and get support.

Clients will always look in their network first, so if you have a big network and are evident in your field, you will find clients seek you out. People hire people they know and like. The more people you know, the more chance you have for success.

Before going to networking events, leverage the personal network you already have. You can practice making connections through your personal network and see where this takes you. After you have done this, you can move on to expanding your reach even more through dedicated events.

Task: In your success journal, write down the names of people you know or people you know of who are connected with a client that you want to work with. Try to get in contact with those people in the next week.

3.3.1 *Networking Events*

Networking events are great for freelancers who are trying to grow their reach. Here, you can meet potential clients, partners, and mentors. These events may seem intimidating at first, but they do not need to be. Really, networking is all about getting to know people on a personal level.

Foster relationships in your network by treating people not as business opportunities, but as friends, knowing that everyone has their own personal goals to meet. Ultimately, it is not about who you know, but who knows you!

You should also be able to tell your brand story in under one minute when networking or introducing yourself.

There are many strategies you can take on to be successful at a networking event. Try some or all of them and see what works for you.

Strategy #1: Start speaking to someone within the first 10 seconds of entering the room. This way, you can beat any nervousness that may prevent you from being outgoing. The only catch here is that you must really open up and force yourself to speak with anyone that has eye contact with you.

Strategy #2: Do not put pressure on yourself to meet everyone in the room. Manage your expectations and focus on making a few solid connections. After all, if you just introduce yourself and rush off, people will not remember anything special about you. Quality over quantity works here!

Strategy #3: Set a time limit (5–10 minutes) for speaking to one particular person. Remember, the goal at a networking event is to meet many different people, not to get stuck in a two hours long discussion with one person!

Strategy #4: Have a "more you, less me" mindset. Ask questions about people and their business at networking events. See how you might be of service to them or connect them with someone you know who might be able to help them. How can you provide value to the people you are chatting with?

Strategy #5: Instead of going into a networking event with the goal of showing off your skills, just go in looking to connect with people. People do business with people they like, know, and trust! Ask questions like, "What do you love? What are you fighting for? What kind of projects do you want to make?"

Strategy #6: Be clear about your business and what services you offer. Use your storytelling skills to give your one minute explanation of who you are, what you do, and why you do it. This way, you will be able to find the types of people you want to work with more easily.

Strategy #7: Ask for leads. If you are interested in working in a particular niche, ask for more contacts from any potential clients you meet.

Strategy #8: Be bold. Clients are looking for people who are outgoing and engaging. After all, if they are at a networking event, they are looking to meet creatives like you. So, take a chance, step out of your comfort zone, and engage with those who really strike you as interesting.

Networking is not just about proving yourself and your work. It is about connecting over common interests and seeing if a particular partnership is worth exploring. If you feel you are not that great at networking in the beginning, do not worry! You will start to feel comfortable and natural in networking environments after some practice. Do not forget about virtual networking session as well.

Task #1: Networking question ideas and planning.

In your success notebook, journal some questions you could ask at your next networking event that would really foster a strong connection. Think about questions that would reveal whether the person you are talking to would be a good person for you to work with or vice versa. These could be things like: What is your favourite type of project to work on? What was your biggest personal success last year? What types of people does your company hire?

Read over these questions before you go to a networking event as a reminder.

Task #2: Be creative in promoting your work and networking. You do not have to limit your networking to specific networking events. What are some conventions you can go to? Are there places for you to speak or teach? Look at the global marketplace, where can you show off your knowledge?

Do some research and try to find at least one alternative networking opportunity that you can attend or speak at within the next month.

3.3.2 *Following-up*

Following-up after a networking event is absolutely essential! People are busy and even if you have a great conversation, they might not remember to reach out to you. Always take the ball in your court and foster a connection by sending an email or a note.

When following–up, there is no need to make a proposition or suggest a collaboration. You can simply say hello and express that it was nice to meet them. Not every conversation needs to be business-oriented.

If you are looking to gain a contact or make a further connection, instead of sending a simple reminder, write an email for the recipient to forward on that introduces you.

Be persistent in your quest to meet and engage with people in your industry. If someone does not get back to you the first or second time, keep reaching out, politely but persistently. This will help you get noticed.

CHAPTER 4

PROTECTING YOURSELF

4.1 BASIC CONTRACTING

When you work for anyone, it is important to have a contract. Even if you are working for a friend, it is important to have an engagement agreement so both parties know what is expected from one another from the start. In our dealings with projects over the last eight years, most of the dispute cases were due to the misalignment of expectations. To ensure a smooth relationship down the road, it is often worth the time and effort to sort this out, so all parties are on the same page.

A contract is an agreement that gives rise to obligations which are enforced or recognised by law and they are always voluntary between two or more parties. Laws exist to protect and regulate both parties involved. Contracts can be spoken or written, complicated and simple. Overall, contracts exist to provide more certainty for both patires and clearly set out the detailes of what was agreed.

As a freelancer, you do not have the protection of a company, a legal department or an HR department. You only have yourself and you need to protect yourself. Contracts are not put in place for those jobs that go by easily — they are there as protection against unexpected circumstances, so no matter what, it is best to protect yourself against what you do not know. A contract will be useful to establish your claims should things go sour and you need to seek a legal route (which should always be the last resort) to settle the disputes. Without a contract, the case will only be built based on what "you said, he said and they said", which is difficult to establish who is in the right or wrong and even if there could be a legal claim.

Different countries will have different legal systems and the contract may vary from country to country. It is important to seek some legal advice to find out the terms used in your local jurisdictions and what some unique conditions you have to include for your own country.

A little disclaimer here for this segment is that the context here is specifically for Singapore. We are not lawyers and the information provided here is purely for educational and informational purposes. Please check with your adviser before taking any actions.

4.2 KEY CONTRACT TERMS

For a simple contract to be enforceable, the key elements that need to be present include:

Counteroffer — When someone proposes changes to a contract. They are not accepting the contract yet, rather proposing a counteroffer. Until there is a middle ground agreed on, there is no acceptance.

Acceptance — The offeree accepts the terms and signs the contract.

Consideration — In legal terms, "consideration" means "what one person gets in turn for doing something." In most freelance contracts, someone is paying money to receive a service. That sum is the "consideration."

Intention to create legal relations — This is the indication from both sides of how serious they are to enter into a binding agreement and to work together. If one side is resistant or refuses to sign, then the agreement will not work.

Capacity — Each side needs to have the ability to enter into a contract. Children under legal age do not have the ability to enter into a contract. Contracts that are signed under the influence of intoxication may not be legally binding.

If all of these conditions have been met, then you have a contract. If any of these things are lacking, then the contract is not legally binding.

Other considerations that you may like to take note of.

- Offers do not last forever and can be terminated in three ways: revocation, rejection, and lapse.
- The offeror must know of acceptance. Silence is not a signal of acceptance!
- The offeror can indicate the mode of acceptance, such as the offeree signing something.
- The price or consideration paid for a promise of work needs to be in the present or future — do not include past debts in new contracts.
- The consideration needs to be a real amount, but it does not need to be adequate to be legally binding.
- Terms in a contract determine each party's rights and obligations under the contract and indicate how these things are meant to be performed.

- Contract terms will also indicate how risks are to be allocated. Who will be liable for any fallout or negative situations that arise from the work done?

It will also indicate how the contract will end, how it could carry on, and how it may be renewed.

<u>Common terms that need to be in a contract are:</u>

Purpose of Contract/Description of Collaboration

What is the aim of the contract?

- Payment/Fees/Consideration
  How much and how payment is to be made
- Rights and Obligations of each party
  What each side is responsible for
- Duration/Termination
  How long will this contract last? When will it end?
- Warranties (this may be country specific)
  These are fundamental promises that the contract will be carried out effectively.
- Dispute Resolution (this may be country specific)
  How are we going to resolve our disagreements?
- The Force Majeure Clause (this may be country specific)
  What happens when unanticipated events occur to disrupt performance?
- The Indemnity Clause (this may be country specific)
  What if one person does something contrary to a warranty?
- The Grant of Rights/Intellectual Property Clause (this would be more relevant to the creative industry)
  Are the deliverables owned or licensed?

- The Confidentiality/Non-disclosure Clause
  How information is controlled and protected — people do not need to know what is going on in your contracts. This protects you and the other party in this relationship.

4.2.1 *Breach and Remedies*

A contract is breached when there is non-performance of a term. This does not mean that the contract is automatically terminated. However, it does entitle the wronged party to demand a cure of the breach from the other party, as well as financial compensation (damages) if there is a loss. They may also be entitled to terminate the contract.

Warranties are what the creator or author agrees to uphold in a contract — for example, that their work will be free from errors and will be 100 percent original. The indemnity clause indicates what will happen if the writer does not perform their warranties. For example, if a third party sues the hiring party for something the writer produces, then the writer may have to take the heat for the work, rather than the hiring party.

A good contract would have some remedies measurement (e.g. mediation) in place in the event of breach. It is helpful to have a clause that indicates what will happen if there is some dispute between the parties in the contract.

4.2.2 *Protecting Your Intellectual Property*

The concept of intellectual property is often a source of confusion for freelancers, but it is vital to make sense of it if you want to protect your creative work.

Intellectual property, or IP, is anything that results from imagination and creativity. A bundle of legal rights protect intellectual property, although protections vary from country to country. Familiarising yourself with IP law is important as a creative because you have legal rights to protecting your work from infringement.

Intellectual property laws recognise that creators have the right to protect their work. These laws allow creators to control and exploit the use of their IP for a specific purpose or period of time. IP is protected as a motivation for creators to keep doing what they are doing. This leads to constant creation and development around the globe. It also allows creators to exploit their works commercially and defend their works from infringement.

The different types of IP are patents, inventions, trademarks, and copyright. As a freelancer, you will mostly be working with copyright.

(a) What is copyright?

Copyright is a form of legal protection that prevents other people from copying your work. Copyright can be described as a bundle of rights belonging to the creator of a work. These rights will vary from country to country. In Singapore, copyright arises automatically; no registration is necessary. Your artistic work will instantly be protected by copyright if it meets the following requirements:

- comes under a category of protection
- is in a tangible form (written or pictured or spoken somewhere)
- it is original and created independently by the author

A copyright clause will set out who will own the work once it is completed. Sometimes the person who is paying for the work will want all the rights to the work and sometimes they will just want to have access to it. Be clear in your contract about who will own the work — this also applies to how you will be able to use it in your portfolio.

How does copyright work for freelancers?

Copyright protects the "form" of an idea, not the idea itself. The law does not aim to limit people reinventing different versions of an already produced idea. Things that are not protected include: (1) ideas and concepts, (2) discoveries, (research findings), (3) procedures, (4) methods, (5) any subject matter that has not been reduced to a tangible form, (6) works in the public domain.

Ideas you have in your head are not protected by copyright. If you have an idea for a storyline or work, be careful who you tell while it is still in idea form! You will not be protected until you have put it into a tangible form. There can by overlapping protections in copyright law. For example, the music in a song and the lyrics are equally protected.

Things created by individuals are protected by copyright for 70 years after their death, after which the work is moved to the public domain. If you pay for a trademark, then your creations will be protected for as long as you pay for it to stay protected. If you create something while you are employed by someone, then the copyright for that work belongs to your employer.

As a freelancer, the ownership of the work you produce for someone depends on what is indicated in the contract agreement. In the contract, it may say that everything you produce is owned by the payee. In other contracts, they may just pay to use the deliverables once, but the deliverables are still owned by you, the author or creator.

If you are commissioned to do a work for someone for a particular reason, then they only have license to use that work for that reason. If they want to use it for another purpose, then they need to pay you for extra licensing.

If there is a group project, where authorship or production is shared, then there is joint authorship.

When signing or using contracts, the IP clause will be important to you as a freelancer. This will indicate who your work belongs to after you create it. Get familiar with the terms "permission", "release", "license", "assignment", and "clearance", as they relate to IP law in contracts.

(b) Buying, selling, leasing, and licensing IP

Intellectual property can be thought of as physical property. You can buy, sell, lease, or license intellectual property.

License is permission to carry out a certain act — therefore a licence entitles the owner to do something with the property it covers. It does not transfer ownership of the property and it allows creators to exploit their work and make money from it.

There are exclusive and non-exclusive licences. Exclusive licences entitle the person who holds it to exclusive rights to its usage (meaning even the creator will not have the rights to it) — whereas non-exclusive licence allows for many people to purchase access to the work.

In legal terms, assignment is how the ownership of intellectual property is transferred. The transference of assignment must be in writing and signed by the assignor. The assignor will lose control of the work and the assignee will gain all ownership and control of the work.

There are several differences between licensing and assigning work. A licence is the right to use someone else's intellectual property, whereas an assignment transfers the ownership of IP from one person to another. A licence allows the owner of the property to still control it, whereas the owner will lose all rights to a work if they assign it to someone else. Licences are generally cheaper than assignments.

In your contracts, your clients may want complete ownership and assignment of the work you produce for them or they may just want to license it for a particular reason.

You can find particular copyright protections for your industry by looking at the **copyright** laws for your country or the country that you are doing work in. If you live in a country that has signed the Berne Convention, you should familiarise yourself with the rights afforded to you on work you do abroad.

(c) How can freelancers protect their work?

The risk of non-payment is often a serious issue for freelancers. To address this problem, you can include in the agreement with your client stating that you will only transfer copyright for your work if you receive full payment and that you will be able to receive credit for the work you have done, so you can add it to your portfolio or showreel.

The grant of rights clause or the intellectual property clause in a contract is the clause that will tell you who owns or controls what.

A license of rights will indicate *how* and *where* the licensee is allowed to use the work.

4.2.3 *Singapore Context*

In Singapore, the Ministry of Manpower (MOM) has set up two tripartite standards for the freelance community. One is the Tripartite Standard on Contracting with Self-Employed Persons (SEPs) which is launched in 2018 in collaboration with National Trades Union Congress (NTUC) and Singapore National Employers' Federation (SNEF) and the other is the Tripartite Standard on Contracting with Media Freelancers driven by the Infocomm Media Development Authority of Singapore.

Businesses which adopt the Tripartite Standard will be listed on the Tripartite Alliance for Fair and Progressive Employment Practices' (TAFEP) website and can use their logomark in their corporate and marketing collateral. This will allow freelancers to identify progressive service buyers and intermediaries, and also help businesses to distinguish themselves.

This Tripartite Standard lends clarity to the expectations and conduct of the relationship. Clearer obligations and duties foster better working relationships between businesses and freelancers and enable freelancers to provide better services. SEPs on their part should fulfil their obligations and duties in a responsible manner.

The written key terms are set out clearly and include the following:

- Names of contracting parties.
- Parties' obligations, such as nature of services to be provided (e.g. outcome; duration; location).

- Payment

    a. Amount of payment due for each product or service (or part thereof).
    b. Due date of payment(s) (e.g. a fixed number of days after the SEP issues an invoice for delivered services or milestones.
    c. Periodic payments for services rendered during that period.

- If terms on variation of the agreement are provided for, how either party can vary the key terms or terminate the agreement (e.g. by mutual agreement).
- If terms for resolving disputes are provided for, the option for mediation should be made available, without it being a barrier to either party bringing any dispute directly to the Small Claims Tribunals.

MOM has developed a form template for SEPs on the key terms of engagement, in accordance with the Tripartite Standard on Contracting with SEPs (TS SEPs). You can check it out on their webpage: https://www.mom.gov.sg/employment-practices/tripartism-in-singapore/tripartite-standards.

Freelancers are also encouraged to refer to the following resources on contractual terms, when generating their own template.

- Law Works Pocket Series E-book on "I want to be a Freelance Professional" from The Law Society of Singapore.
- Advocates for the Arts — A legal handbook for the creative industries from The Law Society of Singapore.

The Tripartite Standard on Contracting with Media Freelancers driven by the Infocomm Media Development Authority of Singapore works in the same manner. The standard outlines four areas for companies to provide in order to deal with media freelancers.

1. Written Contract

A written contract between contracting parties are agreed upon and acknowledged before the commencement of the service. The written contract includes the following terms.

   i. Names of contracting parties
  ii. Nature of services to be provided by the media freelancer/s
      a. Details of services that include deliverables, e.g. duration, location
 iii. Payment
      a. Breakdown of fee
      b. Payment milestones with clearly specified payment schedule
      c. Amount of interest to be charged for late payment calculating from the agreed payment milestone, upon the company's receipt of the invoice from the media freelancer/s
  iv. Ways both parties can vary or terminate the contract terms
   v. Types of information to be kept confidential
  vi. Disputes will be settled via negotiation and mediation first
 vii. Where relevant, clear terms on ownership of intellectual property

2. Timely Payment

Media freelancers are paid in accordance with the agreed payment period upon payment milestones being met as stipulated in the written contract. If no payment milestone dates are provided in the contract, the media freelancers are paid, no later than 45 days upon the company's receipt of the invoice from the media freelancers, upon completion of agreed deliverables.

3. Dispute Resolution

If any disputes arise in relation to the provision of service by the media freelancers, reasonable efforts are made to resolve the dispute via negotiation and mediation first. Any agreement reached during negotiation and mediation will be recorded in a written settlement agreement and acknowledged by the parties involved.

4. Insurance

Where media freelancers are required to offer their services on set and/or location specified by the company, they are covered by the company's insurance. A suitable liability insurance will be purchased.

   i. Production Equipment Insurance that covers equipment operated by media freelancers either owned by the company and/or rented to the company
      a. Covers against all risks of direct physical loss, damage or destruction to equipment such as cameras, electrical communications, sound, lighting and grip equipment that are owned by or rented to the company
  ii. Commercial General Liability
      a. Covers against claims for bodily injury (of other parties, e.g. passersby who are injured by production equipment during production that was operated by media freelancers) or for property damage, liability arising during the production
 iii. Work-related Personal Accident insurance

It is important as a contract worker to be familiar with contract law. You should familiarise yourself with the terms and law specific to your country. When you sign a big contract with a lot of money involved, it is a good idea to take the contract to a lawyer to make sure everything is fair and balanced.

4.3 INSURANCE

Insurance for entrepreneurs and everyone for that matter is risk management. In life and in business, there is some risk that cannot be accounted for and avoided. As a business owner and operator, you can mitigate risks to your business and livelihood by buying insurance.

When you decide to buy insurance, try to cover all the bases, from catastrophic health issues to loss of property. If your insurance can mitigate all risks, then you will be ready and prepared for anything.

In this section, we will go over all the different types of insurance generally offered. The names of insurance may vary by where you live and where you buy your insurance from. Also, as a disclaimer, we are not financial agents and hence the following does not constitute any advice of any sort. Do speak to a financial agent in your country who will be able to better advise you on insurance policies that would be suitable for you and your business based on your need and budget.

Even if you are just starting out and have no money for insurance premiums, look into what you can build for the future. This will give you goals and contribute to your business plan. As your business grows, you will have more at stake to protect.

4.3.1 *Personal Health Insurance*

As a freelancer, no one else is going to be paying for your health insurance. It is up to you to value your health. Health insurance is an important part of setting yourself up for success in your business and your life. Some countries and freelancer unions offer special programmes and rates for freelancer health insurance.

Note: If someone hires you for a job that is high-risk, such as filming at a dangerous site, you can ask for more money or for them to insure you.

In some cases, having your own insurance may make you much more marketable, especially if you are in a particularly risky line of work, such as a wildlife photographer.

4.3.2 *Income Protection Insurance (Disability Insurance)*

Depending on what country you live and work in, you may be eligible for income protection insurance (sometimes known as disability insurance) for freelancers. This is another important part of health insurance for freelancers. **Consider this:** if you fall sick or have an accident, you will not be able to work. When you are a freelancer, there is no such thing as sick leave. Your clients are not going to pay you for any time you are not working. Income protection insures you for the time you were unable to work, so you still have an income for that time.

4.3.3 *Commercial Property Insurance*

Property insurance covers any property that you use to run your business. If you require equipment to run your business, you should definitely consider insuring your equipment. If you are a writer, then your computer is of utmost value to you. If you spill coffee on it one morning, how will you make money the next?

With property insurance, you can insure individual items or your office.

If you have an office, consider getting office (contents) insurance. Office insurance will cover any equipment that is in the office. If you need to, then you can also get individual insurance on the things you bring out of the office.

If you have a lot of equipment and have insurance, you can let companies know they do not have to worry about anything if there is an accident, because you have insurance. Let them know that when you prepare your invoice for them, you will charge a small amount for insurance during the time of engagement.

Note: While it is certainly important to have insurance, also consider your premiums. If you are spending your entire pay cheque on your insurance policies, it is not sustainable. Consider only insuring the things that you cannot replace or supplement with something else.

4.3.4 *General Liability Insurance*

General liability insurance covers you, should anyone be hurt on your property or as a result of something you or your property did. It also covers you against libel, slander, and copyright infringement.

It may not seem necessary but imagine this. You work on a logo for a company that has given you very specific requirements. Later, they are sued for copyright infringement because the logo looks just like their competitors'. You were just following instructions, but your client can still sue you for their losses. General liability insurance will cover your costs.

4.3.5 *Professional Liability Insurance (Professional Indemnity/Errors and Omissions Insurance)*

Professional liability insurance covers your legal costs should you be sued by a client for damages or losses caused by alleged negligence in your work. These types of cases require mass amounts of money to sort out, and this insurance will cover those expenses for you.

Let us say your client is an advertising agency that is delivering a huge advertising campaign to a top-tier company. You are doing the video editing for the advertising agency, but you miss your deadline because you have a three-day migraine. Because you have missed the deadline, the advertising agency has too. The top-tier pharmaceutical company pulls out of its contract, and the advertising agency loses thousands. They decide to sue you for their losses. Professional liability insurance will cover your legal bills from the proceedings.

This type of insurance is often held by contractors and consultants. It may seem like a silly thing to get because you feel your work is impeccable, but remember, insurance is there to protect you from *unforeseen* complications.

Mitigating your risks as a freelancer and an entrepreneur is an important part of running a successful business. Other types of insurance you can consider include:

- Commercial auto insurance (if you use your car for work)
- Cyber liability insurance (protects against losses from hacking)
- Business interruption insurance (should a natural disaster prevent you from working)
- Hospitalisation Insurance
- Personal Accident Insurance
- Equipment Insurance
- Life Insurance

Most often, insurance plans can be bundled together to save the buyer money. Take a look at all your options, what is recommended most where you do business, and consult with your union if you are a member (they will most likely offer discounted rates).

4.4 TAKING CARE OF YOUR MIND AND BODY

A lot of freelancers may neglect their most important assets which is yourself. It is especially important for a freelancer to take good care of your mind and body, otherwise you will burn out very soon.

4.4.1 *Stay Positive*

Throughout your career, you will inevitably run into defeats, failures and hiccups. As an entrepreneur, it is important to stay positive through these difficulties. It is possible that you will be your only cheerleader when it comes to business, so you may need to learn how to motivate yourself and keep going despite failures.

4.4.2 *The Practice of Positivity*

As with everything, staying positive is a practice. Here are some things to remember as you move through difficulties in your career.

Remember your vision. Hold onto that dream you have for yourself and let that be your motivation to keep going.

Have patience for yourself and your business. You will not be able to build your network, your business, and your brand overnight. These things take time. Hang in there!

Stay persistent on your path. Your steps do not have to be big ones, just keep moving forward and expanding your knowledge.

Be okay with being mediocre at the beginning of your career. Your quality would not be the highest at the start. It takes time to grow. Keep your goal in mind, and work tirelessly towards it.

Cultivate a habit of following through with things. Successful people follow through with their plans. All you need to do is start and stick to it.

If you cannot impress your client, impress yourself. Not everyone will love your work 100 percent of the time, but you can do your personal best 100 percent of the time.

Give yourself praise. If you are doing what you love, you are already lucky. Take time to appreciate all that you have built. Be proud of it. Taking time to see how far you have come will help you realise your future goals as well. Working as a freelancer does not have many of the high communal moments of success that working on a team or in an office will have. When your clients are pleased with your work, take that opportunity to be proud of yourself.

Learn from your down times. Look at your challenges as opportunities to learn and grow not only as an entrepreneur but as a person. Think about what these down times teach you. How can you bring this emotion and humanity to your work?

Remember that failures are stepping stones. Failures are part of life and the business of freelancing. You will not have the support of a team to help you get over these failures, so you must learn to look at these failures as learning opportunities, rather than setbacks. Let them roll off your back and keep going no matter what.

Have an outlet to deal with stress. Freelancers do not have co-workers to turn to blow off steam. Learn proactive and healthy ways to deal with stress for yourself.

Reflect on stress. If you are super stressed out about something, take the time to step back and view it from a bigger picture. Have you learned something from it? Will these small mishaps matter in five years?

Be flexible with others. As a freelancer, you are constantly working with people you do not know. This requires a lot of patience! Instead of becoming resentful or stressed by working habits that you do not jive with, choose to stay relaxed. Learn to let the small things go and calmly stand up for things you really believe in.

Stay connected to your passion. What is the biggest guarantee of success? Passion! If you are passionate and excited about what you are doing, it will be hard to fail. Surround yourself with things that fuel your passion, whether it is motivational books, others' work or personal inspirations.

See market downshifts as opportunities. There will always be downshifts in markets, or challenges in our respective industries. And there will always be people making money despite it all. So, be positive and creative about ways you can use these dips to your favour.

Always do your best. No matter what job you are doing, do your best. The level of your product should always be up to the highest of your standards. Keep your brand value high, no matter what you are getting paid or what the project is. This will keep you from missing opportunities or regretting.

As a freelancer and an entrepreneur, you need tenacity. It is important to decide that no matter what happens and how long it takes, you will be successful. Positivity is a choice. Each day choose to look at the bright side of things.

Task: Find a stress-reliever.

What are some things that you do that really help you relieve stress? Think about a list of possible stress diversion tactics so you already have a plan in place when you get in over your head.

CHAPTER 5

KEEPING YOUR CLIENTS HAPPY

5.1 FINDING CLIENTS

At the beginning of your career, it may seem daunting to try to find new clients. However, everyone has to start somewhere. Even if you are new to freelancing, there are ways you can find clients to build up your client base. Here are some strategies you can adopt to start finding your first clients.

Strategy #1: When looking for your first clients, look to your immediate circle of people you already know. Even if your immediate circle does not have any jobs for you, maybe the people around them do. If you want to work in a certain industry or circle, find out where those people hang out. Start networking by being social.

Strategy #2: Offer your take on an existing product of a client you would like to procure. Submit your suggestion for them. This puts you on their radar — even if they do not hire you right away, they may call you when they need a redesign later. You are showing potential value to them and adding to your portfolio.

Strategy #3: Go on job boards. You will most likely have to apply to many to get a few responses, but this is still a great way to build your portfolio. Eventually, some of these will be converted into long-term clients and you will be growing your network.

Strategy #4: Offer helpful advice where and when you see fit! Where can you offer your advice online? Can you respond to Quora questions? Could you write an article on LinkedIn? If you can teach a potential client something, then you automatically have value to them.

Strategy #5: Be known in the industry you are in. Comment on other people's articles and make your opinion (politely) known. This will also portray you as an expert and put you in people's awareness.

Strategy #6: Reach many people quickly by offering bulk deals to everyone in an association. For example, you might offer to create websites for every teacher at an art school. This is faster than approaching, one at a time.

Strategy #7: Work with a freelance agency. In some industries, you can work with a freelance agency that can find you work based on your skillset.

Strategy #8: Go to networking events. Use these events to make real connections with people and foster opportunities for work.

Strategy #9: Be reliable. If your work is always on par and you always message clients back within a reasonable amount of time, you will catch the work you want. If you are not there to receive it, it may pass you by and go to someone else.

Strategy #10: Use online freelancing and online networking platforms (which include social media groups). These platforms provide solutions to the common problems that freelancers face, like collecting payment and securing clients, but at a cost. At the beginning of your career, paying this price might be well worth it. You can consider approaching us at CreativesAtWork as well. However, we have our own in-house onboarding process for the selection of freelancers.

Getting your first and second clients will be the most difficult! You may have to offer to do some work for free to build up your port-folio and gain testimonials. However, if you are good at what you do, once you gain a few clients, the rest will come more easily. In the beginning, stay focused and start with a handful of clients. Once you learn to handle five or six clients, add more slowly.

Task: Before you go out to find clients, think about who you want to work for and make a list — part of this includes how much money you want to make. For example, if you want to make SGD$500 an hour, you should not shoot for charity clients.

The ideal clients to look for are in industries or for companies you like, that are accessible, and that pay for things. If you do not like the companies you are working for, you will end up hating what you do. If you only shoot for jobs in insider industries, you may never get work (at least in the beginning). If you only want to work for companies that generally do not pay for things, you will not get paid! The sweet spot exists in the middle of these three things.

Think about who matches all three of these criteria and interests you. Write them down in your success journal.

5.2 PICKING PROJECTS

Part of being a freelancer is having the freedom to choose what you want to work on. What you choose to work on will greatly direct your career, so it is important to take some time to consider which jobs you want to take on.

When you are entering the industry, know that you do not have the experience everyone else does. Be okay with learning for a while, for taking projects on for less money than you might want or doing things you might not be so passionate about. You might not see something as super beneficial to your career or profitable, but you never know what a project might teach you or bring you in the future. In the beginning, it is all about learning.

Taking every opportunity that comes up, in the beginning, will give you the experience and exposure that you need. As your business grows, you can become pickier and begin to think about opportunity loss. Everytime you say yes to something you say no to something else. Make sure you are making a life, not just a living!

You may need to become a master of balancing jobs that pay the bills and jobs that feed your passion. Both are important! Recurring and regular paying jobs can be considered your "core work." However, the successful freelancers that we see may not be the most creative or artistic but one thing that they all have in common, is good business senses.

5.3 DIFFERENT TYPES OF CLIENTS

As you get hired for different jobs in your freelancing career, you will run into many different types of people with many different management and work styles. As a freelancer, you would need to be able to deal with different types of management styles, you should have some idea on how to handle the more difficult clients.

The following are some more common types of "difficult" clients that we have come across.

(a) The Micromanagers

If clients micromanage you, try to understand why they are micro-managing you. Possibly they do not trust you, they do not trust anyone, or they just have that type of personality. Once you find out which one of these it is, you can learn how to address it.

There are a few ways to deal with clients that micromanage you. One way is to establish a strict schedule and stick to it. Sometimes micromanagers have a fear that you will not deliver what you said you would. If you establish a schedule and update them frequently, then hopefully they will begin to relax.

If clients are crossing the line with their micromanaging, you must be honest with them, but be tactful always. A candid discussion will go a long way in building up a good relationship.

(b) The Oblivious

Oblivious do not know what they want, they do not know the ins and outs of the industry or their heads are in the clouds. If you have clients like this, you must be very patient and use simple terms with them. They need to be reassured that they are being treated fairly. It may take extra time to communicate with them. Try to:

- Use terms and examples that they can relate to. Do not use long acronyms or technical jargon to confuse them further.
- Use pictures and visual aids to illustrate your points. This is incredibly useful because it reinforces the authenticity of what you are saying and promotes trust.
- Write it all down and take the efforts to go through them. Work out a comprehensive contract with them to help them feel

secure. They may not understand the details of your work, but they do understand a fair deal.

(c) The Know-It-Alls

These clients want control and respect. You must give them control, respect, and an occasional compliment. When you strongly believe in something, remind them that you are the expert in your area and hold out for that. Let the small stuff go, it is not worth your worry!

But do give them an occasional compliment. A Know-It-All will be much more inclined to accept your proposals if their input and ideas are appreciated. Also, you will have to pick your battles. Do not fight on every little issue; save your strength for when the critical moments occur.

(d) The Cheapskates

Start high when you are bargaining with cheapskate clients. If they bargain you down, they will be happy, and you will still have a good price for your project.

During a project, work quickly for clients who are cheapskates. The project price will not be high, but if you can fit your work in a faster time, you are not wasting time and money. Make sure in your contract with them, you clearly state the deliverables and deliver nothing more. If not, the next time, they will ask you for more things.

(e) The Dreamers

Sometimes clients want things that are not possible, out of budget, or will take too much time. When dealing with these types of clients, you must have a very clear idea of the scope of the project and have a set timeframe as well.

Without putting them down, you must bring the dreamer back into reality. Let them visualise and interact with your work to help them better understand the scope. Always bring them back to what the project objectives is and the brief that you have received.

Ask them to show you examples so they can do some reality check themselves and hopefully, they realise that it cannot be done.

Be straightforward with prices and timeframes. Sometimes what the dreamer wants is not impossible, it is just difficult. If that is the case, give them a solid price and timeframe to do the work in. Remember, do not say "no" immediately without giving them a chance to share with you their thoughts. Instead of saying "no", can just candidly share with them your current constraints and the challenges you foresee that will come up if this happens for example, will there be security issues, will it involve seeking clearance with another level or another organisation, etc.

Ask them about the details. Dreamers rarely fill in the blanks. While their end goals are usually incredible, sitting down with them and discussing the details can help both you and they get a good grasp on the scope of the project.

(f) The Wiggle Room Takers

You may have clients who try to slightly alter the end date of a project or the deliverables in such a way that you feel you do not want to discuss charging them more. Just be aware that this is a slippery slope — they may change it slightly many times and take advantage of you!

(g) The Enthusiasts

These are the clients that want to help you and will assist you in your job. If you say "no", it might ruin the relationship. So, allow them to do the things they want, but make sure they have the skillset. Let them know if they do not and gently remind them that this is why they hired you.

The enthusiasts want to be involved in the work. They carry with them a lot of enthusiasm that needs to be released in a constructive and practical way. If they want to assist you, then give them that opportunity.

- **Give them tasks.** Let them assist you with some of the simpler tasks which can also save you time and money. Be sure to identify your client's skillsets before assigning them the tasks.
- **Ask them to research.** Whether you use the information they find or not, research tasks can keep an enthusiast out of your way and give you the time to focus on your job. They could also provide an alternative perspective on the information gathered.

(h) The Underlings

The underling is the guy who is not the boss — he cannot make the decisions, so you have to educate him and trust that he will get the info to their boss. Read between the lines to find out what the boss wants — not what the person talking to you wants. You will also have to prepare and expect to buffer for time. What the underling wants does not really matter — what matters is what their superiors want. Ultimately, if the work you give the underling pleases their bosses, you will have a very happy client. The key to dealing with an underling is to think like an employee. Strategically plan ahead for the "let me get back to you" mentality when working for an underling.

- **Ask questions in bulk.** Individual questions get lost in emails and sticky notes. The best way to save yourself time and stress is ask all questions possible in one go so you do not waste time emailing back and forth.
- **Prepare for the lag.** Do you know how news reporters always take a minute to respond to questions? This is exactly what you will have with an underling. Ask questions ahead of time so you are properly equipped for the next phase of your work.
- **Do not bother explaining.** If you are working for an underling there is a good chance their boss is the next type of client on our list. This means that the underling just needs to know the highlights of the work you have done because that is all their boss wants to hear.

When dealing with difficult clients, remember that they are just trying to get their job done too. They have asked you for help because they need it, not because they are trying to make your life difficult. Of course, some clients will be really enjoyable to work with! How well you work with someone should be a sign to you of how you want to continue the relationship after a project is completed. Remember, you can fire your client! This is one of the best perks of freelancing. If someone treats you badly (does not pay on time, does not respect your time, etc.), stop working with them!

5.4 KNOWING YOUR WORTH

First: never associate your self-worth with your price. Making less does not mean you are inferior as a photographer or graphic artist — there are many factors that determine whether a prospect accepts your price, and you are not the only one.

A prospect may love your work, but not have sufficient budget. Or perhaps they were ready to pay your price, but an economic situation caused them to delay the project.

If your price is rejected, *it is not necessarily a reflection of your worth*. Do not overreact by dropping your prices to rock bottom.

That being said, how do you price yourself? There are a number of methods.

- **Find out how much your peers make and position your prices accordingly.** This is easy but not always possible; in some industries, like writing and design, there is no real "standard rate."
- **Decide how much you want per hour, and price according to that.** If you want to make at least SGD$70 an hour, and a project would take you 10 hours, your price is SGD$700.
- **Price per project.** This is not advisable for new freelancers, who may not be clear on how long a project can take. More seasoned freelancers — who can gauge the commitment required — may just charge a flat fee per project, which many clients prefer (variable costs are harder to plan for).
- **Go on commissions.** You may be given a commission, such as a cut on everything sold via the website you build for the client. Make sure you have an accounting process if you choose this kind of payment — who has access to the sales records, and what happens if products are defective or returned?

5.4.1 *Pricing Structure*

There are many different ways to price your services. First, you need to figure out how much you need to charge hourly to achieve your goals and maintain your company structure.

Step one: Look at your goal sheet to see how much you want to make in your first year and then add a small amount for emergencies.

Step two: Figure out what your costs of doing business annually are. Think about web hosting, Internet, project management tools, software, marketing and insurance… all of these things add up quickly!

Step three: Calculate your cost of living. Make a specific list of your annual costs such as rent, mortgage, groceries, transportation costs, medical bills, etc.

Step four: Add all of these things together to see how much money you need to survive for one year.

Step five: Figure out how many billable hours you will have in one year. Calculate how many hours per day you want to work, how many days a week, and times that by 52 weeks a year.

Step six: Then, give yourself some time off! What kinds of vacation time are you looking for? How many sick days do you want to give yourself? And how many public holidays do you want to take off?

Step seven: Subtract your total time-off from your billable hours to figure out how much time you actually have to work in a year.

Step eight: Out of those working hours, many will be spent on business operations, like marketing, invoicing, and all your other business management issues, rather than actual projects. So, take about 25 percent off the top of your billable hours to figure out how much time you will actually have to work on projects.

Step nine: Divide all the money you need to survive by your final billable hours. All of this will determine your hourly rate.

Step ten: Every couple of years, re-look at your rates and consider raising them as you become more experienced.

There are many ways to charge per project, which we will discuss later. However, this hourly rate should be your guide, as you never want to be making less than this. As you progress through your first projects, ensure that you are getting paid enough to sustain yourself and meet your goals.

5.5 PITCHING, PRICING AND NEGOTIATING

Pitching and negotiating are two skills that freelancers need in their toolbox to be successful. If you are an excellent pitcher, you can find and take on jobs of your choosing, and if you are an excellent negotiator, you can always get paid what you are worth and more.

Let us see how we can be great at pitching and negotiating.

5.5.1 *Pitching*

Freelancing and pitching go hand in hand. Even if you have a solid network and can get client referrals, it is important to know how to pitch properly. Pitching is a great skill to have because it ensures that you will always have work if you do it well. As you may meet any potential clients at anywhere anytime, hence it is good to make sure you are always prepared; you need to be ready to let your pitch loose at a moment's notice when you stumble across a prospective client. Pitching is an important tool to help the freelancer to land more jobs and build up a sustainable freelance career.

It is always good to prepare an elevator pitch on hand about your-self and your services as you will not know where and how you will meet your potential clients. It could be at your son's sports event, it could be at a networking session or even at a seminar. While preparing your elevator pitch, do keep the following in mind.

- Keep it short (Not more than two minutes)
- Conversational (No jargon)
- Keep it conceptual (No time for details)
- Focus on the what (Not the how)
- Inject storytelling element
- Tailor your pitch to your audience

Another simple way of preparing the elevator pitch is to answer the four questions below.

- Where have you been?
- What is your professional journey?
- Why are you here?
- What do you bring to the table?

If the pitch is pre-arranged, make sure that you do your homework first. Research and have some knowledge when going into a meeting or sending an email. Speak about what you believe in, what is the obstacle your clients face, and what your solution is. Help your potential clients see how you are going to add value to their business and overcome their obstacles.

Do not be afraid to talk about how you execute your projects. If you include all the little details of your work, you will show off your expertise and the client will understand why you are worth your price.

If it is applicable, include a series when pitching. For example, if you are a writer, you could propose to a hotel chain that you will write a series of articles about the best date night ideas in their city for each month. If your series is popular and has a following, they will want to keep you to retain this following.

One way to pitch successfully at a higher price is to switch your pitch from being task-oriented to being value-oriented. What goal can you help the company achieve? How are you helping them get their reach?

Note: If you are pitching specific work to a client, issue a non-disclosure agreement to protect your intellectual property.

5.5.2 *Pricing Schemes*

Although your per hour rate should guide you, especially in the beginning, there are many different ways to charge clients.

(a) *Charging by the hour*

When freelancers are first starting out, it is difficult to know how long a project will take. For this reason, it is often best for new freelancers to charge by the hour. This way you ensure you estimate too low and have to do work at a very low rate. It also ensures that you will get paid for any changes in the project as it progresses.

However, it is more difficult to earn higher amounts for jobs when you charge by the hour.

When charging per hour, you may have to face two undesirable questions: (1) How much work can you really do in one hour? (2) Your number is so high, why are you worth that much?

You will have to prove your value to clients, and they will have to trust that you will work at a rate that is acceptable to them. When charging by the hour, it is more difficult to charge by value because you are putting a price directly on your time, rather than on the benefit to the customer.

(b) *Charging by the project*

Project billing is great if you can work quickly and accurately, so this is great to move towards to after you have some experience. You can get paid more for your time by charging per project.

When charging by the project, estimate how long a particular project will take you and then times that by your hourly rate. Then, add in a couple more hours to cover unexpected working hours and other expenses, such as cost of meeting with customers, running your equipment, and self-funded benefits (insurance, accounting, marketing, etc).

Project billing is not always based on your hourly rate. You can quote higher and tell the client that you are worth a certain price. For this, you will have to show the value that you are bringing to their company.

It is possible that you could underbill if you work more slowly then you first estimated or if there is a change in the project scope. When the work changes, you are entitled to raise the price of the project, but if you are not good at customer service, this part may be difficult for you.

When doing project billing, consider charging 50 percent or 100 percent upfront. As a small business, cashflow is important to the company so you should not delay all the payment toward the end.

(c) *Value-based billing*

Another way to price your services is by value. If a website for a customer is going to make them a million dollars more a year, then you should be able to charge a considerable amount of that value.

Doing value-based billing requires you to understand the market and be confident in your services. Try to quantify the value you are proposing as much as you can. You will begin to understand how to do this later on in your career when you have seen how much your clients benefit from your services.

Remember, sometimes values are intangible. The things you provide such as awesome customer service, industry insights and connections, are also of value, so charge for them. Ensure that you highlight these things when proposing your rates.

When you sell this way, clients will tend to overlook your competitors and buy your value rather than an hourly or project–based rate.

There are also other ways to charge clients, such as charging a day rate, which is great for more consultant types, for equity, which is great when you are working with start-ups, and by commission, which is good if the value you bring to clients is easily quantifiable.

Charging by the hour will be the easiest first, but as you progress in your career, you will find it easier to sustain yourself by charging by value.

5.5.3 *Negotiating*

Negotiations can be difficult at first. Your mindset before going into negotiations is especially important. Remember that you are an investment, not an expense. Speak from a place of power and remind your clients of the financial upsides that you will be bringing to them. Help them see your value. Switch your pitch focus from task to value. It is not about how much this task should cost, but how much value you will be bringing to the company.

However, negotiation requires both parties to be agreeable to give and take. Be willing to negotiate with your clients and potential clients, on timelines, prices, and deliverables. You want them to do the same for you.

When entering into negotiations, it is okay to ask directly about a client's budget. If clients do not have specific numbers in mind when discussing their budget, you can ask for ballpark numbers. Then, you at least understand what you can quote. However, it is possible that they will quote you something very low and you may need to walk away from a project. For this reason, many leaders in the industry recommend making the first offer when negotiating.

It is very hard to get a price higher when the client makes the first move. Propose high and give yourself more wiggle room. But of course, if the client is also doing an open call, if you quote too high, you may not be considered as well. Hence, you need to find out as much of the project as possible, so as to decide what is your next move.

Things to consider when quoting prices.

- To figure out a project rate, look at the scope of the project. Conservatively estimate the number of hours it will take you, and multiply those hours by your hourly rate, add any working expenses and add a few extra hours for buffer.

- Charge 20–30 percent above average for your services. You are not getting employee benefits and you deserve to be compensated fairly for your excellent work.
- Ask clients questions about what their goals are for this project. Do they want to grow their reach? Do they want to grow their sales by 1 percent? Tell them how you can assist them.
- Outlining the phases and the cost of each phase can be amazingly effective. It is reassuring for the client to know you have a plan and understand what is needed.
- Think about what value you are bringing to a company, not just the skills you bring to them. Are you helping them expand their reach? Are you helping them convert sales? Your value to your client is not just your base skill — just by having better customer service than your competitors, you are of higher value. What can you do that makes you more valuable than anyone else?
- Consider if you like the client when taking a job or quoting a price. It is possible that some clients are not worth the fee or your time.
- Think about how much you would expect the client to be able to pay you. If you are working for a corporate client, you can expect them to be able to pay you a bit more. If you are working for a start-up or a small business, you can expect them to pay a bit less. Quote accordingly.
- It is best to have an extremely specific scope of work in the beginning. That way if anything changes within the project, later on, you can negotiate a higher price.
- Know what your priorities are. Be transparent about what is important to you and ask what is important to them. This prevents you from wasting time.
- Know your walkaway price from the beginning. What is the bare minimum you will take for a job? If your client cannot meet that, you know that you will walk away unless it is a marketing decision.

- Be confident. To charge what you are worth, you need to believe you are worth that price. If you suffer from self-doubt, your client will read that in your tone and body language.

Of course, no matter how well you pitch, sometimes your clients will not be able to meet your price or will want to counter-offer. Or, they may go quiet for a reason unknown to you. What are some ways to deal with counter-offers and quietness professionally and easily?

- Behave like the expert that you are — if you do not know an answer to a question, find out. Do some research or tell your client that you will get back to them.
- When clients put pressure against you saying you have to "do better," do not cut your prices. Keep your stance and reiterate your value to your clients.
- It is better to avoid cutting your rates, and instead cut the scope of work. If a client tells you they cannot afford your fee for the job scope discussed, you can offer to change the job scope. For example, if you quote USD$10,000 for a 10-page website, but they can only have the budget for USD$8,000, offer to do a six-page website for USD$8,000.
- Do not negotiate with yourself and cut your own rate if there is silence on the line. Send a follow-up email, but never cut the rate before they get back to you about it.
- Never go lower than the price a client offers you, especially a corporate client. They would expect you to take the higher price and consider yourself worth the higher price. It could actually damage your relationship if you take a lower price.
- Do not give clients things for free unless it is part of your strategic marketing strategy. If you start to give clients things for free, they will start to devalue your work and time. If it is based on goodwill, make sure the client knows that you are offering complimentary due to goodwill, however, they cannot expect the same again.

- Sometimes, clients may dance around a particular issue and not talk straight. It is okay to ask to get the conversation back on track.
- If a client asks you to do something you know cannot be done, for whatever reasons, offer solutions. If you can show that you offer more than just execution, but consultation, your value goes up.
- Ask questions and really listen. If there is a block, something that is preventing you from moving forward, find out what it is so you can address it.
- If a client is a super aggressive negotiator and does not want to give you anything that you ask for, keep your ground. Remember, you are an asset.
- It is okay to walk away from negotiations. At some point, you may realise it is not worth your time or worry to make a project happen. When this happens, walk away.
- If a client walks away from a negotiation, let them. If you try to chase over them your rates may be pushed down. If you want to contact them again, wait a month or so.
- When a client tries to reopen points after an agreement has been made, do not give in. They will keep pushing, so take a firm stance right away and politely call them out for breaking the agreement.
- After an agreement has been made, never tell a client that you would have done a job for less. It does not reflect well on you and if they hire you again, they will not want to pay you more.

If you are charging by value, clients do not care about how long the project will take you to complete, all they care about is if the work is done well, and within the agreed timeframe. If they benefit from the quality of the work in a tangible way, they will pay you what you charge.

Remember, it is okay to lose clients if they are unwilling to pay you what you are worth. People of honour value effort contributed and pay for work done.

As your experience being a freelancer grows, your rates will as well. This inevitably means that you may have to raise rates for existing clients, and they may not be able to afford you anymore. It is your choice whether it is worth it for you to maintain the relationship and undercharge them.

5.6 GOOD CLIENT RAPPORT

5.6.1 *Before Starting a Project*

When you step into the freelancing market and start working for different clients, you will quickly find that your clients have many different ways of communicating and handling business. As opposed to an office job when you work with mainly the same people all the time, you will be working with different people all the time.

This requires flexibility from you, but there are also some best practices for dealing with clients. Here are some of the guidelines you can adopt for client relations before starting, during, and after completing a project.

#1 Have the Correct Documents in Place

Always ensure you have a **contract or written engagement agreement** with your clients, so you can refer to it if any issues come up.

Contact reporting guidelines is a document that will outline when and how you will report your progress to your clients. These can help your clients rest assured that your work is progressing on schedule and that you are serving them well.

Project briefs are documents that summarise the services and timelines a project entails. These can minimise the risk of misunderstanding between you and your client and accelerate the efficiency of deliverables.

#2 Manage Expectations

Usually, conflicts arise between clients and freelancers when the clients have unrealistic expectations of freelancers or they do not really know what they want to begin with. Make sure that everyone is on the same page before beginning.

To get a clear project scope, ask the following questions: What is the goal? What is the timeline? The budget? Who are the stakeholders at each stage? What are the deliverables required? Project briefs, reporting guidelines, and contracts will all help with this.

In the creative world, it is sometimes not so easy to be clear about what has been completed has not been successfully and what has not been completed. Be clear in your communications about the specifications and keep a written record of them. Indicate in your agreement how many revisions you include in your initial price.

You also need to manage your own expectations. If you are on the production side of things, you may often have to deal with clients' budgets restricting how you work.

Tip: Finding it hard to figure out what your client wants exactly? Try asking them if they know what they *do not* want.

#3 Keep a Record of Everything

To ensure you and your client are always on the same page, keep notes on conversations. Then, include a brief summary of them in an email so you can refer back to them should any discrepancies arise. If there are any instructions that have been passed down and differ from the brief, be sure to document it down in email and get the client to send you confirmation in black and white.

Likewise, save all emails, notes of conversations, files, and instructions sent to you so you can have a record of what was asked of you! This will help should a client ever complain about your work.

As you are the expert in your area, not your client, they can easily overlook information that is necessary for you to complete your project successfully. Make sure to ask questions for clarification in the beginning.

If you follow these steps from the beginning, you will avoid disputes and miscommunications with clients and your projects will have a much better chance of going smoothly.

5.6.2 *During the Project*

How you handle your clients while a project is ongoing will have a huge impact on your success as a freelancer. Clients love to work with freelancers who are attentive yet independent. They want to know how your work is going, but they do not want to hold your hand while you work on a project. Remember your role is to help them to do their job better. If you can integrate yourself into their team, you will enjoy a long-term relationship with the client.

(a) Communication

As a freelancer, one of your main responsibilities will be communicating with clients during the implementation of the projects. Open communication and mutual understanding between you and your client will lead to trust. This, in turn, can lead to long-term relationship. How well you communicate will dictate how your clients feel about working with you and how smoothly your projects go.

You will be exposed to many different communication styles from clients. Of course, some clients are not good communicators themselves! Learn to be flexible with your ways and modes of communication, while being as clear as possible yourself.

Being in contact with your client about the progress of your project is one way to keep things going smoothly and to keep everything on track. You can let them know all the steps you have completed so they can see how much work you have put into the project.

If a project is broken down into milestones and your client signs off on each one, then it limits the possibility of them rejecting large pieces of your work, asking for reworks, and disputing the level of work.

Hint: When communicating with your clients, use "we." You are part of their team and this gets them used to thinking of you as a member as their team.

Task: If you have clients currently, do a quick check of all your communication lines. Could you be nicer? More thorough? More respectful?

(b) Winning Long-Term Clients

When you obtain a client, you want to keep them as long as possible. There are certain things you can do to retain as many clients as possible during the project:

- be positive
- be a useful resource
- accept personal and cultural differences
- stay in contact
- provide notification of delays

- always be civil and honest
- create boundaries
- reward your loyal clients

Converting one-off project owners to ongoing work is easy and formulaic if you can get into a habit of it. You do not need to think of every client as a unique challenge in terms of converting them to long-term clients. There is a formula you can use for each one that is the same.

Simply put, you need to understand your client, what their business needs are, and propose further plans to fit their needs. Let us break down all the ways in which you can do this.

- **Think like an owner**

This means you can put yourself in the shoes of the business owner and understand their needs. You can show your ability to think like an owner and be valuable to your client by meeting them regularly, once a week if possible, to discuss their problems and needs. Come to these meetings with one or more suggestions for them.

Another way to do this is to be a radar for industry news. If you stay on top of industry news and standards, you can educate your clients. In this way you become more than just a freelancer, you become a valuable consultant.

- **Understand your clients' broad goals**

Usually, clients will express their linear goals or short-term goals to you. They will tell you exactly what they want you to do. However, if you understand what they need in the long term, you can suggest what type of content they need in the future.

- **Turn out quality work, without fail**

People will forgive you if your work is slow but good — you will lose clients if you are turning out deliverables that are not high quality.

Strive to deliver the best, all the time. If for whatever reason you are late in submission, do give early notice to your client and let them know instead of "disappearing".

- **Qualify your client by telling them why you are happy with them**

This shows you understand them and see the work that they are doing. It also shifts some of the power to you — it shows that you have a choice of who to work with. If you do this, clients will remember you!

- **Be a connector**

You become valuable if you can connect your clients with each other. One thing that distinguishes freelancers from employees is that freelancers know different people. Your reach is wider than the average employee.

As a freelancer who works with many different people, you can be a centre point for clients to meet other people in their industry. Do not be shy about introducing clients to each other.

- **Get to know your clients' customers**

If you put your name on your work and your clients' customers know you, make it a point to get to know them. The closer you are linked with your clients' customers, the more your client will want to retain you.

- **Ask questions during meetings**

When you are in a meeting with clients, show that you understand and are listening by asking questions. This also reduces the times you need to take their time by emailing them for clarifications. This is important — your clients are busy and if they can trust you to work independently, they will value you.

You can also ask questions that show your expertise. If you ask questions your client has not even thought of, you show you are the expert. For example, if you are a writer, you can ask how many times they want you to include keywords in the copy for search engine optimisation (SEO) purposes. If they have not even thought of this, then they will really consider you an expert and feel the need for you.

- **Discuss missed goals**

Talk about made and missed goals with your clients. If you had a goal to reach a certain number of followers and you are not going to make it — bring it up. You can then sit down to talk about a different strategy, and this gives them a chance to keep you on longer.

- **Explain your work in detail**

If a client asks you how you do what you do, explain in extreme detail all the work that you do. If they can see how hard you work and all the dedication you put in, they will be happy to pay you for it. If it overwhelms them — they will know they cannot do it themselves.

- **Be a problem solver**

Freelancers who know how to solve problems are extremely valuable to their clients. They become almost invaluable because, without them, the client's problems are not going to get solved.

- **Dress the part**

If you are going to meet a client, make sure that you are dressed the part of the expert, especially if the meeting is at their office. If you are going into a formal corporate setting, look like a business professional. If you are heading to an office of a start-up where freedom in the workspace is a big value — wear what you would like. Just be aware of and respect the company culture. Even if the meeting or discussion is conducted online, just because you are at home, does not mean that you can dress up as if you just woke up. Dressing well is also a form of respect for the client.

- **Be reliable and accountable**

Always set clear expectations and live up to them! Be proactive at your work and always meet your deadlines. Clients love to work with freelancers who are reliable, available, and in touch.

- **Under promise and over deliver**

If you can impress clients, again and again, they will always come back.

- **Be invested**

Clients can feel when you are interested and invested in a project. Are you just passing hours in a day? Or are you dedicating your time and talents to be a problem solver and executor?

- **Be a team player**

If you can be cost-effective and work well with an established team as an outsider, you will be desirable for long-term projects.

- **Reward your clients**

You can reward your loyal clients by sending something small to thank them. You can also send them holiday cards or other small gifts.

If you can learn to keep clients for the long-term, your career in freelancing will become easier and easier. Your working relationships will grow, your clients will value you tremendously, and hopefully, you will be working on projects you really enjoy. Having long-term clients also provides a level of security and stability for your freelance career. You do not have to spend too much time looking for new clients at the expense of doing "real" work. However, having said that, as a freelancer, you still need to allocate some time to do marketing and soliciting of new clients as you will not want to put all your eggs in one basket.

If you do keep your clients, limit the number of new clients you accept. You only have a certain amount of time in the day, so ensure that you are not stretching yourself too much and it affects your quality of work.

(c) Resolving Issues

When working on projects, inevitably, there will be some hiccups along the way. If you can learn to bend and flow with these hiccups, you will be resilient in your career. Of course, these things are not ideal but learning strategies to overcome obstacles is part of running a successful business.

Here are some strategies for resolving issues.

When you need more time

If it is just a day or two, ask the client for an extra day to polish your work instead of disappointing them by missing the deadline.

If you are going to miss a deadline by longer than a day or two, make sure you let your client know as soon as possible. It may not even be your fault, but it is important to let them know so they can make any adjustments they need to.

When clients ask for extra revisions

"Can I get this done in one minute?" Ask yourself this question when thinking about doing an extra revision for a client free of charge. One minute of work could earn you a returning client. However, you do not want your clients to begin devaluing your work.

When a client has an issue with your work

In case of a conflict with a client, make sure you acknowledge their concerns. Sometimes people just need to be heard. Understanding your clients' needs and fears while at the same time asserting yourself will help you solve problems effectively and with ease.

Avoid public shaming — disputes are bound to happen sometimes, but you should always respond by taking the high ground and seek mediation rather than publicly shaming someone or talking bad about the clients!

When you are wrong

Over the course of your freelancing career, you will be wrong sometimes. It is important to acknowledge your mistakes when these things happen. Offer solutions, learn and move on.

When discussing mistakes with a client, never get defensive! As a professional, you should never take things in business personally.

When your client is wrong

If an issue comes up and the client fails to see where they are at fault, it is okay. Remain as professional as possible and try to find a solution.

Likewise, as an expert in your field, it is okay to disagree with your clients sometimes. They have hired you to be the expert, so if you know a better way to get something done, speak up!

Remember, if it comes to it, you can fire the client! You do not have to continue to work with people you do not mesh with.

The main thing to remember is to be flexible and respond to issues that come up without reacting. Instead of making rash decisions, use your creative energy to come up with solutions. When your client sees that you are devoted to finding the best possible answer for everyone, their trust in you will grow.

Flexibility should be part of your engagement agreements, as well as your mindset. Every project has unexpected issues and concerns that come up. Learn to be agile with yourself and with your clients.

When clients go quiet

In the case of a client losing contact or going quiet, stay calm and do not assume anything. Sometimes clients go quiet because there are changes on their end and they feel stressed at the thought of cleaning up the process. Do not assume that silence on the line is anything to do with you.

Never act desperate with clients — they will feel this and possibly lose respect for you.

If a client goes cold, simply hold them accountable for what they said they would do, while still being polite. Try something like, "I'm confused, you said you... Has something changed?" This will keep them accountable and will sort out the issue right away.

You can also offer them options to continue or not. This will get the conversation back on the fast track again.

However, when clients go cold, it is possible that you sold something wrong — try to figure out if that is the case by asking them if something changed. Do not take it personally and try to address it.

5.6.3 *After Completion*

How you wrap up your projects with your clients will also affect how many clients you retain as long-term clients and how you get referrals. Always ask clients for feedback on your communication, productivity and work. You can start to find out what clients like best about working with you and use that when marketing your services.

After a successful project, do not be afraid to ask for referrals. You can even write a draft of a referral email and ask them to forward it on for you. Usually, happy clients will not mind doing this for you, but they probably will not think to do it unless you ask.

Pay attention to your clients' needs after you complete a job. Understanding what is next for your client is an important aspect of your job. With this knowledge, you can either offer to help or pass along information to the next person who will touch the project.

As your own boss, remember to reward and encourage yourself after you do a job well done. Give yourself a pat on the back when completing projects.

5.6.4 *Handling Rejections and Criticism*

No one likes being rejected or criticised, but in this business, you will have to learn how to deal with criticism. Not all criticism is created equally — some criticism is constructive; some criticism is simply the result of different tastes. It will be up to you to see clearly which is which.

The first step is to learn to take criticism and not take it personally. Remember that everyone has different tastes and they are not blanket opinions of your work or your value as a creative.

When you do not take criticism personally, it allows you space to not get aggressive or defensive. Instead, ask questions and see what you can learn from or where you can try again. Remember, we learn more from our failures than our successes.

If something goes really wrong, never lie to a client. Come forward openly, honestly, and as soon as the mistake has been made. If you break trust with a client by lying to them, it will be extremely hard to gain their trust again. It is always best to be straightforward and honest.

Resolve any issues with clients in private, right away. Getting a negative review online could potentially destroy your reputation in seconds.

Sometimes, you will see that criticism from clients is not helpful or constructive. Sometime, they may not even know what they want. Know that any abuse coming from clients is not worth your time. Learn to cut the cord and walk away to protect yourself if things get ugly.

Of course, handling rejection and criticism will naturally be hard. As creatives, we must face the music of how our work falls on different tastes and styles. Especially when we take creative risks, rejection can be heart-breaking. However, even when something stings, do it anyways. Learn to live with heartache and learn to move on from it. From your persistence will come your best work.

If you cannot impress your client, impress yourself. Not everyone will love your work 100 percent of the time, but you can do your personal best 100 percent of the time.

5.7 TRUSTWORTHY

A big part of your ability to price yourself is based on trustworthiness. Clients do not like to take gambles on important projects. If you prove yourself reliable, most will rather come back to you than try out someone new.

Staying trustworthy means:

- **Meeting deadlines or advising on delays** — Do not make a habit of missing deadlines. On the times, when you must miss deadlines, inform the client early. Communicate clearly as to when the work will be delivered.
- **Do not steal business** — For example, if you are a freelance copywriter for an ad agency, do not offer to work directly for the agency's clients. You *will be caught*. If you are doing something that could be considered stealing business, be graceful and talk to your client about it — you may be able to formalise things with methods like a referral fee.
- **Do not reveal confidential information** — Do not gossip about your clients to the public, or to other clients. If you are going to write about a client's project, be sure to get permission first.
- **Respect non-compete clauses** — Do not work for two or more clients who are competitors. Most will have a non-compete clause in contracts to prevent this. But even if they do not, avoid conflicts of interest by working for competitors (you may consider doing so after a project is done, and if the non-compete clause would allow it).
- **Do not lie about who does the work** — If you were paid SGD$2,000 to design a logo, do not pay a student SGD$50 to do it for you. If you are a writer, do not outsource the writing to a ghost writer. The client is hiring *you specifically* — you are the one they want for the job. If you are going to outsource, get their approval first.

5.7.1 *Building Good Rapport*

Good rapport means repeat business. It also means clients are more willing to refer you to others and will speak well on your behalf. Freelancers do not get far without good testimonials, and nothing beats word-of-mouth referrals.

You can build good rapport by:

- **Jumping in socially** —You may not work in their office. But that does not mean you cannot join them for lunch now and then, or send a Christmas card.
- **Respecting corporate culture** — The fact that you can wear shorts to their office does not mean that you should. If your client has a formal dress code, be respectful of it when visiting.
- **Following up** — On events like New Year, do connect with old clients and ask how things are going. Do not become another forgotten contract worker.
- **Giving clients leads when they appear** — Sometimes, you will meet people or businesses that could be important to past clients. Be sure to refer them; your former clients will appreciate it.
- **Do not bad mouth them, even when the project is over** — Perhaps the project was tough, or they were hard to work with. But what do you gain by complaining to the public? Do not burn bridges if it is not necessary.

5.8 CONSTANT UPGRADING

Staying relevant in your industry means continuously upgrading your skills, staying on top of industry standards and moving with the times. Being proactive about these things is important for freelancers because no one is going to tell you that you need to do these things. It will be expected of you, and if you do not measure up you will not stay in the game.

5.8.1 *Upgrade Your Skills*

If you feel you are being held back from performing at your optimal because you do not have the skills or the expertise to do so, it may be time for you to invest in upgrading your skills. This could be anything from taking an online course to going back to school. Remember that technology is changing all the time and even if you are very good at what you do, there is surely something you have not learned yet.

However, since you will not get paid when you are not working, plan your times for upgrading strategically. When choosing how and where to upgrade your skills, consider the most efficient and shortest ways to do so. Think first about the ways in which you could expand your knowledge and skills without taking time off. Plan for it so that you do not go through any serious financial dips.

5.8.2 *Stay on Top of Industry Standards*

Understanding industry standards means that you are clued into what is going on in your industry. You know the newest things happening and you can share them with your clients.

How do you do this? Be part of a network within a community, share with others so they share with you and follow industry news on blogs and social media accounts. The more involved you are with your industry, the better known you will be anyway. In this way, you will become a specialist or consultant as well.

5.8.3 *Move with the Times*

With technology growing all the time, many freelancers find themselves overwhelmed or out of their comfort zones. You do not have to be an expert in everything, but you do have to keep yourself growing with the rest of the world.

Technology enables us to learn different skills and gives us more access to different operations. Due to the proliferation of knowledge in today's world, many clients are expecting their freelancers to be able to do more and more. Do not be surprised if you are asked to use a wide range of skills when working on projects. If you are in film, you may be asked to be the producer, director, and editor. As a business owner, consider what is most beneficial to you — becoming a specialist or a specialised generalist.

Another way technology is changing the gig industry is through sharing and rating systems. Embrace this and look for new ways to leverage technology, social media, and crowd sharing platforms to elevate your business.

In the end, staying relevant is all about finding a way, your way. You do not have to utilise every new trend but stay informed so you can decide what is best for your business.

CHAPTER 6

GOING GLOBAL AND MOVING FORWARD

6.1 MAKE YOURSELF AS MOBILE AS POSSIBLE

6.1.1 *Working Across Borders*

One of the coolest things about being a freelancer is that you can easily work across borders. Your client pool is not just limited to those who are in your country. As office and work cultures vary across the globe, you will need to have some cross-cultural sensitivity when working with clients from overseas. It is a good idea to familiarise yourself with the customs and communication styles of the country of your clients, it is always good to have some basic understanding and see how you can best fit into their culture.

(a) Working with Overseas Clients

Before taking a job overseas, do some research and consider what are the challenges you will face? Ask yourself about your technical requirements for the job and if you have what it takes to complete the assignment and provide value to your overseas client.

Some questions to ask before taking an overseas job.

- **Will you have access to everything you need to complete the job?**
  Find out what is needed for you to work remotely. How is the brief or meeting going to be conducted? Who should you work with or consult if you have any questions? What languages are they using for communication?
- **What are the local customs?**
  When working on an overseas project, it is necessary to know about and respect local cultures and customs. It is possible that these things may affect your work also. You may need to dress differently or avoid working on certain days.
- **What language is spoken? Will you need a translator?**
  For certain jobs that require a lot of collaboration with local partners, you may need a translator. Even if your partners speak good English, some official documents may still need to be professionally translated. This cost should be considered when discussing terms with your client.

You should discuss all these things with your client before you take on an overseas job. However, remember that as much as you can plan, there will be some things you cannot foresee. For this, you need to be as flexible as possible and be ready to think on your feet to solve problems. Cultural considerations need to be exercised at all times.

After you complete a job overseas, reflect on the tools you needed and how is your working experience with the overseas client. This will help you plan future overseas jobs and contracts.

6.1.2 *Working Remotely*

Working remotely can be unnerving. It requires a lot of trust from both the client and the freelancer. Developing your cross-cultural communication skills will help ensure that you are always on the same page as your foreign clients.

When working with clients from around the globe, take special care with your communications, understanding that some ways of speaking and collaborating will be different than what you are used to. Make sure to take time to understand job descriptions and expectations, as you may run into cultural and language barriers.

When communicating with partners overseas, especially those where language might be a barrier, always summarise your conversations in emails. Having written records will help both sides be sure of what is expected of them and can clear up any uncertainties or possible misunderstandings from phone conversations. If you have requirements from your clients, include them in all communications, so they are not missed or overlooked.

When giving or receiving feedback to/from your foreign clients, remember that not all cultures have the same conventions you do. Something you may consider to be rude may simply be straight talk in another culture. Likewise, something you feel should be easy to discuss might be more of a hush–hush topic in other cultures. Be careful and considerate with your wording, noting these possible differences.

6.2 DIGITALISE YOUR SKILLS

Digitalisation will happen at a speed and scale that we never see before affecting almost all sectors from education, health, finance, etc. It is no longer just good to have, it is a must have for survival for freelancers. Digital skills will be critical for freelancers both in terms of reaching out to more customers for ourselves but also, for our clients in helping them to reach out to their clients. It is an important time for freelancers to assess our strengths, sharpen our skill profiles and think about new products and services we can offer.

Key digital skills are required as more businesses ramp up their digital presence. Some of the areas you can consider include online marketing/lead generation tools to increase deal flow as the economy stabilises, coding, web development, content creation or marketing are good skill sets to have so that you can develop to boost your own business or help your client's to boost theirs. Understanding SEO and how different social media platforms work would help you to stand out amongst your competitors.

6.3 KEEP MOVING FORWARD (KEEP LEARNING)

Throughout your career in freelancing, you need to be willing to upgrade your skills and continue learning about your craft, industry and business ownership to stay relevant. If you assume that you know everything there is to know and stop learning, you will quickly lose your edge and competitiveness.

Be willing to learn. This requires you to be humble and admit there are things you do not know, but the truth is, even the highest of CEOs do not know everything. You can always make your best better.

Let us look at some ways freelancers or entrepreneurs can do to keep learning.

Choose projects that teach or challenge you: When choosing between different projects, think about what would teach you the most. Which would push you to the next level with your skills?

Try new things: Do not be afraid to do ground-breaking things, especially in your passion projects. Push your creativity outside of its box. Trying new things is the main way we learn. Even if you fail, you will gain new insight and knowledge.

Find a mentor: As a freelancer, you will not have the guidance of bosses or trainers to help you grow. Seek out others you admire in your field and learn from them. If possible, get a mentor who will be willing to help you develop.

Get feedback: Getting feedback about your ideas and projects is one of the best ways to learn what works and what does not. Ask your mentor, previous clients or other creatives to critique your work. However, build good discernment about who you listen to about your work. Getting constructive feedback is good, but you still want to maintain *your* essence.

Work with different types of people: As a young freelancer, you may need to work with older freelancers on projects, likewise, if you have been in the game for a long time, you will have to learn how to work with younger freelancers. Learn to bridge the gap by understanding each other's strengths and weaknesses. Older free-lancers will have more knowledge of the industry as a whole, while younger freelancers will understand how newer technology and media work.

Upskill: Expand your skill set all the time, and never become com-placent! Markets are growing all the time and you have to grow with them.

Be curious: If you really love what you do, you will be successful because you will always be finding ways to grow. Be curious about your industry and entrepreneurship in general. When you have passion to keep learning, you will constantly be propelling yourself towards success.

Multiple streams of revenue: As a responsible business owner or freelancer, one important factor to consider is to explore how we can build multiple streams of revenue rather than just rely on service or commission fee. We need to constantly think creatively and do our research, you can find some ways to monetise your business online: whether you are a small business setting up a virtual store, or a freelance professional breaking into creating online courses and content for the first time. Do not forget to constantly look for ways to create multiple revenue streams.

The most important element in learning is to stay passionate about what you do. Many clients would rather hire freelancers who are passionate rather than skilful — even if you are not the most skilled at first, you will definitely develop your skills by being passionate. If you are humble and willing to learn, you might find that companies are willing to teach you and help you along in your journey.

Remember, even the most experienced people do not know everything, so stay humble and open to new knowledge.

CONCLUSION

The freelancing journey is not easy. As freelancers, we need to constantly stay nimble, be flexible, adapt to changing demand, and innovate accordingly, so as to maximise our business' potential. Amongst our pool of freelancers, we witness that the top 20 percent will be able to build a sustainable business and have a constant supply of jobs. And amongst the top, only a handful (around two to three-percent) go on to establish their company or agency and are able to transit from an individual professional to a business owner.

Although the journey is challenging, the accomplishment and fulfilment is irreplaceable. We have created this book to document the key considerations and pitfalls of being a freelancer to help more to succeed. It is our mission to *help freelancers who want to continue freelancing to be able to do so.*